The Saint Book

THE
SAINT BOOK

*For Parents, Teachers, Homilists,
Storytellers and Children*

by Mary Reed Newland

illustrated by the author

A Crossroad Book · The Seabury Press · *New York*

1979 · The Seabury Press · 815 Second Avenue · New York, N.Y. 10017

Library of Congress Cataloging in Publication Data

Newland, Mary Reed.   The saint book.
"A Crossroad book."
SUMMARY: Brief sketches of more than 55 saints,
arranged by the dates of their feast days, focusing on
personal details and factual incidents of their lives.
1.   Christian saints—Biography.   [1.   Saints]   I.   Title.
BX4655.2.N48   282'.092'2 [B] [920]   79-16457
ISBN 0-8164-0210-8

For someone who once said to me,
"I do love saint stories.
I intend to be one myself, you know."

Contents

October

November

December

Why These Saints?

The saints included in this book are here almost by accident. Originally it was to have contained the lives of all the saints in the lectionary, the almost 200 who have an official feast listed among the liturgies for the year. But that would have created a dictionary with a short entry for each one—date of birth, date of death, a few lines too general to be of any use—and no one would have been served. What I wanted to do, I suppose because I always wanted someone to do it for me, was a book of stories of the "saints of the day," dependable enough to be trusted and with a good tale or two so they would be useful to families, teachers, homilists, or anyone curious about the saints and interested in them again after the past decade or two without them. A whole generation has grown up without knowing the saints, a generation which thinks they belong in the category of fairy tales and myths but sometimes asks: "Were they *real?*" They certainly were real, and not to know them, whatever one's age, is to be a deprived child.

So the saints for this book have been taken from the

lectionary but there has been room for only a few for each month. Choosing them was a random thing, like going to the market and seeing such an irresistible display of items that one says, "Oh, I'll take this one, and this one, and of course *this* one." And then, discovering how many great saints are not in the lectionary, like Brigid of Ireland and Joan of Arc, I added some of those. Before I knew what had happened, there were enough. Many favorites are left out simply because there was no room for them, and I confess that there are a few I didn't know quite what to do with so I looked the other way.

What I discovered in the process of all the digging and reading and thinking that goes into two or three pages of text is that in the end people are saints for the way they love. Every so often someone pleads that we leave the saints on their pedestals and stop trying to make them seem like us, but I cannot agree that to find them as human as the rest of us does a disservice to anyone. After coming to terms with the humanity of Jesus, to leave the saints floating about on clouds makes them irrelevant even to him.

Some saints, I suppose, never said a cross word, held a biased opinion, or gave way to an explosion of wrath or a bout of depression, but it is encouraging to find that so many did. More power to Vincent de Paul, who acted like a lamb most of the time even though he had a bad temper and was impatient and irritable. It has been said we could go to hell imitating the faults of the saints, which is true, but St. Bernadette cried out, "Don't tell me their virtues, tell me their weaknesses and how they overcame them!" Me too!

Jerome would never have made it through today's canonization process with its fine combing for faults. He was irascible, and in paroxysms of penitence he beat his poor bony breast with a rock until it was bloody. He could get along with no one but women, apparently, who alone could "gentle" him after those venomous explosions at everyone in sight who disagreed with him. But he loved the Word of God so passionately that he translated it into the common tongue for folks like us.

Catherine of Siena, who is claimed as a kind of early women's liberationist, was not concerned with the plight of women but totally and passionately with the plight of the church. She simply saw what needed to be done and plowed ahead, in a fashion enormously admired by her followers and infuriating to her adversaries. For Catherine, as for Brigid and for Paul, in Christ there is no male or female. The church has still to learn this.

It is interesting, after all these years, to read of the saints' predilections, of the kind of company they were attracted to, and the beauty and Christ-likeness of their love. It leads me to believe that some gay people have been saints—or should one say some saints have been gay? Whether they had gifts or lacked them, were brilliant or poor theologians, reached the heights of mystical asceticism or practiced bizarre penances, it was the way they grew in love that was the key to the way their faults and weaknesses were consumed. Even Benedict Joseph Labre, who cautioned his family to meditate constantly on the pains of hell because "so few are saved," could say in the end that were he to be warned by an angel before his death that he would be damned, he would still have confidence.

Along with everything else, reading the lives of the saints makes it clear that as a community, the church has gone through stages of conscience and moral growth much as humans do. There are saints who supported the Crusades, like King Louis of France, and like Catherine of Siena who thought a Crusade would help to reunite the disparate factions in the church and bring them to singleness of purpose. Fortunately, it never got started, and today there is nowhere a Christian who would countenance such an undertaking or even defend the past with all its ghastly bloodletting and throat-slitting of Jews and Saracens. There are saints, it is true, who refused to go to war; and then there is Joan of Arc who led troops under, she said, the specific command of God. Today not only the whole church but the whole world struggles to find ways to stop war and create peace.

Not knowing all the answers is not an impediment to holiness. What is required is nicely told in a little story from the *Lives of the Desert Fathers* which goes like this.

The abbot Moses asked the abbot Sylvanus, "Can a person every day make a beginning of the good life?" And the abbot Sylvanus replied, "If a person works hard at it, he can begin the good life all over again, not only every day— but even every hour."

Good. Here I am—and it is now a quarter of two. . . .

I am grateful to the library of the College of St. Rose in Albany, New York, for the help of their staff and the use of their fine collection. Thirty of these lives appeared first in *The Evangelist,* the newspaper of the Diocese of Albany, New York.

Mary Reed Newland

January 4

Saint
Elizabeth Seton
1774–1821

E lizabeth Ann Bayley, one of two daughters of a prominent Episcopal family, was born in New York on August 28, 1774. She was a charming little girl, small-boned and dainty, with great brown eyes and a face like a cameo, who from the very first loved God and wanted to be good. Having lost her mother at the age of three, she was deeply attached to her physician father and used to sit beside her schoolroom window watching for him on the street. When he appeared, she would slip out quickly and run for a kiss. As a young girl, she experienced the ups and downs of adolescence, imagined now and then that her father did not love her (there was a stepmother), and on one melancholy occasion she fantasized ending it all. She rejoiced in the world on one day and on the next longed to retreat to a convent in the country to teach children about God, or to join the Quakers "who wear such pretty bonnets."

Beautiful, vivacious, fluent in French, a fine musician, and an accomplished horsewoman, she grew up and became a popular guest at parties and balls. Long afterward

· 1

she wrote of all this as quite harmless, except for distractions at night prayers and the bother of fussing over dresses. Small wonder young William Seton fell head over heels in love with her. She returned his love adoringly and they were married, surely to live happily ever after.

It began felicitously enough in a gracious home on Wall Street, William busy at his family's shipping business, Elizabeth with the beginnings of a family. Anna Maria was born, then young Willy, and then came a thin thread of worry in the form of William's ill health. With the death of his father, their fortunes began to decline. William was tormented by visions of debtor's prison, while Elizabeth was certain that God would help them to survive. "Troubles always create a great exertion of my mind," she wrote, "and give it a force to which at other times it is incapable. . . . I think the greatest happiness of this life is to be released from the cares of what is called the world."

In two and a half years, they were bankrupt. Elizabeth spent that Christmas watching the front door to keep out the seizure officer. The following summer she and the children stayed with her father, who was health officer for the Port of New York on Staten Island. When she saw the babies of newly arrived Irish immigrants starving at their mothers' breasts, she begged her physician father to let her nurse some of them since she was weaning her fourth child, but he refused. By summer's end, he too was a victim of the yellow fever epidemic, and Elizabeth was grief-stricken. More and more she turned to the Scriptures and the spiritual life, and in May of 1802 she wrote in a letter that her soul was "sensibly convinced of an entire surrender of itself and all its faculties to God."

Then in 1803, the doctor suggested a sea journey for William's health. Against Elizabeth's better judgment they set sail for Italy to visit their friends, the Felicchi family. To pay for the voyage, she sold the last of her possessions—silver, vases, pictures, all probably inherited from her father. The voyage was pleasant, but arriving at Leghorn they were quarantined in a stone tower on a canal outside the city because of the yellow fever epidemic in New York. There she endured for forty days the cruelest suffering she was ever to know, possibly the key to all that happened during the rest of her life. She wept, then reproached herself for behaving as though God were not present. She tended the racked patient, now coughing blood; amused Anna Maria, who had come with them, with stories and games; and held little prayer services. When the cold numbed them beyond bearing, she and Anna Maria skipped rope. William died two days after Christmas in Pisa, at the age of thirty-seven. Only the laundress would help the young widow to lay out his body.

While waiting to return to America, Elizabeth attended the churches of her Italian friends where she was deeply impressed by the Catholic belief in the real presence. If this teaching about the Blessed Sacrament had been held in the Episcopal church in New York at the time, Elizabeth Seton's story might have been very different, for this doctrine was at the very heart of her conversion. Returning to New York, poor now and living upstairs in a little house supplied by friends, the news of her interest in the church stirred up consternation on all sides. She agonized with indecision about it until finally, on March 14, 1805, she became a Roman Catholic.

Several plans to support her family failed, and finally she opened a boardinghouse for schoolboys; but when her sister-in-law, Cecelia Seton, became a Roman Catholic also, her angry supporters withdrew. Hearing of her need, the president of St. Mary's College in Baltimore offered her a residence with a teaching position in that city. She accepted and left New York for good on June 8, 1808.

In March of 1809, she pronounced her vows before

Bishop John Carroll of Baltimore, was given some property in Emmetsburg, Maryland, and in June she, her three daughters, her sisters-in-law, Cecelia and Harriet Seton, and four young women who had joined them, began what was to become the American foundation of the Sisters of Charity. For special occasions they wore black dresses with shoulder capes, a simple white bonnet tied under the chin (like Elizabeth's mourning dress); and for everyday they wore whatever else they had. Their temporary abode provided four rooms, two cots, mattresses on the floor under a leaky roof where in winter snow sifted down over them. Vegetables, now and then a bit of salt pork or buttermilk, and a beverage called carrot coffee was their fare—all flavored with that great zest for survival which had become a habit with Elizabeth. When they moved to their unfinished permanent home they were invaded by fleas which had infested the horsehair for the plaster. Finally the home was completed and they had "an elegant little chapel, 30 cells, an infirmary, refectory, parlor, school, and workroom."

But once again death became a familiar. Harriet died, then Cecelia, and torrents of invective from New York condemned Elizabeth as "that pest of society, that hypocrite and bigot." In the eleven years left she would lose Anna Maria and little Bec (Rebecca) as well; her grief over the loss of her loved ones was long and terrible.

But life went on. The rule, money troubles, possessive clergy, an ill-suited spiritual director, additional schools, the demand for more and still more sisters, were only some of her burdens. Through them all she seemed to remain cheerful and patient, but her letters to her director reveal the terrible suffering, the aridity, the darkness of soul. Her sons, upon whom she doted, were ordinary, self-centered young men whose faults their mother never saw quite clearly. Until the end of her life she sent them money, proposed schemes which did not appeal to them, wrote them sentimental letters, and worried for their souls. William eventually married (one of his sons would become a bishop); while Richard, having been spiritually adrift and in debt, returned home, rectified his life, signed on a merchant voyage, and died at sea. Catherine, her youngest child, became a Sister of Mercy in New York and lived to be ninety-one.

Elizabeth Seton died slowly and painfully of the tuberculosis which had stricken all her family. At the last she was sustained on nothing but a little port wine. She had written to her best friend not long before, "I'll be wild Betsy to the last." The night of her death, January 4, 1821, she began the prayers for the dying herself, and one of the sisters, knowing that she loved French, prayed the *Gloria* and the *Magnificat* in French with her. The spirited young woman who had wanted only to marry a handsome man, be a happy wife, and raise a pretty family, had had adventures beyond her wildest dreams. Loving by nature, she grew in faith and hope because of trial, not in spite of it. And with each trial God revealed resources, strength, and courage she did not know she possessed. We call it coping—and we need a patron saint for coping.

January 5

Saint John Neumann
1811–1860

B ishop John Neumann of Philadelphia was so unimposing in appearance that Archbishop Bedini of Thebes, visiting the United States, reported him to Rome as ". . . a little inferior for the importance of such a distinguished city, not in learning nor in zeal nor in piety, but because of the littleness of his person and his neglect of fashion . . . the populous City of Philadelphia, rich, intelligent, full of life and importance, surely merits a bishop of another type."

For all the archbishop's snobbery, John Neumann would have agreed. He *was* little—five-feet-two—neat though shabby, with a broad pleasant face, a much abused hat, and sturdy shoes for journeying about a diocese which extended far beyond fashionable Philadelphia. Once, returning from a visitation with wet feet, it was suggested that he change his shoes. He admitted that if he did, it would be to put the right on the left and the left on the right, since he had only one pair.

He was born in Prachatitz, Bohemia, on March 28, 1811, and from the very beginning was a good child who had a horror of offending God. He was whipped for the first lie he ever told, and he never told another. As a young man he was so in awe of the priestly vocation that not until his mother persuaded him did he finally enter the seminary, where he distinguished himself with a brilliant scholastic record. Attracted to the missions of German-speaking Catholics in America, he quietly began to prepare himself by practicing stringent mortifications—going without food and sleep, and staying up entire nights in the sharp autumn air. He studied French, Spanish, English, and Italian (he already knew German, Czech, Greek, and Latin). Years later he would add Irish when he discovered that many Irish immigrants to Philadelphia could not go to confession for lack of English. (One old woman was heard to thank God joyfully, as she emerged from the confessional, that at last they had an Irish bishop.)

Two disappointments greeted him upon graduating from the seminary. Because of the illness of his bishop he was not ordained, and his application to the bishop of Philadelphia remained unanswered. Although his family grieved to see him go, he left one frosty winter morning in

1836 with forty dollars in his pocket, no certain destination, and a passionate conviction that he was called to serve in America.

Fifty days crossing Europe by stagecoach brought him to Paris where he lived like a pauper and waited in vain for news from his various applications. One month later, with a few modest possessions and his precious books, he boarded a three-masted schooner and was on his way to America.

He set foot on Manhattan Island after forty days, his clothes in tatters and with one dollar left. Making his way to Bishop Dubois of New York, he learned that he had been accepted for that diocese, and within a month he was ordained. He set off for Buffalo by Hudson River, train, and Erie Canal, stopping to celebrate his first Mass in the Church of St. Mary, in Albany, New York.

In Buffalo, Father Neumann, the younger and stronger of its two priests, chose the outlying half of the area. For his lodgings he had a garret room in a local inn; for his church a half-built stone edifice, roofless and windowless. One time, bigoted townsfolk threw shovelsful of mud and manure over the wall and narrowly missed hitting the altar as he pronounced the consecration.

With a heavy pack on his back, he covered miles of wilderness, slogging through the snow, rain, and mud to exhort, encourage, minister, heal, anoint, bury, shrive, celebrate Mass, and officiate at weddings. He cared for the Irish, French, and Scottish scattered among his Germans, and taught their children not only religion but reading, writing, and numbers. And there were dangers. One night he was mistaken for a corrupt local politician and a mob evidently tried to lynch him. He was found lying unconscious in a ditch with a rope around his neck. Another time a band of Indians found him collapsed on the road, sick with fever.

In the winter of 1839–40, knowing that he needed the support of a community if he was to survive spiritually and psychologically, he was admitted to the Redemptorists. His novitiate, to which he looked forward with joy as a time of silence and prayer, was spent in Pittsburgh where the demand for German-speaking priests filled these precious months with parish duties. Next came Rochester, Buffalo, Ohio, but he blessed it all as "the will of God." And then he was told, "Report to Pittsburgh as superior."

He went, and this was an end to his freedom. Months later an order came from Belgium which made him general superior of the American Redemptorists. He wept. It meant enormous responsibilities—schools, parishes, the governing of men many years his senior, begging money, acquiring sisters, much more. His only hope lay in intense prayer and an impeccable observance of the rule. "Do not *seem* superior," St. Vincent de Paul had said to the superiors of his own congregation, and John Neumann never did. His room was a tiny cell, his wardrobe empty except for one habit.

In 1851, the see of Philadelphia was empty and John Neumann was nominated to fill it. Hearing this, he went on his knees before the presiding bishop and in tears begged that the recommendation be changed. He hurried about the city to convents and schools asking prayers for his "special intention," and he wrote to his superiors in Europe asking them to discourage Pius IX from choosing him—in vain. In fifteen years the penniless seminarian from Prachatitz was bishop of the largest see in the United States.

He lived nine years longer, to build more schools than any bishop in the country, to found teaching orders of nuns, to visit parishes (one time he rode on a manure spreader in a country district). He write a German-American catechism and, in time, offered to divide his see in two, taking Pottsville as his own, but he was turned down. He gave himself away, after the counsels of the Gospels, and died exhausted on January 5, 1860, at the age of forty-nine. One little old lady said after his death: "Oh, to see that humble little creature you would never think he was a bishop."

Saint Antony of Egypt
251–356

Most people know St. Antony of Egypt best from paintings of him as an old man being tempted in the desert. In error chronologically (he was young at the time of the temptations), they depict him as menaced by lurid creatures who so outnumber him that a viewer might well wonder if he survived. But survive he did, and nicely, until the age of 105, and became known through all of Christendom as the first of the Desert Fathers and the founder of western monasticism.

The *Life of St. Antony* by his friend Athanasius is the source of all we know of this saint and, while not a biography in the strict sense, it was written around a nucleus of historical fact. Set forth for the edification of the faithful in the style of the ancient writers, its delightful mixture of marvels and wisdom presents as touching a portrait now as it did when it was first written.

St. Antony of Egypt was born into a Christian family in the village of Coma in middle Egypt in 251 and was a solitary child who preferred to remain at home rather than play or go to school. At twenty, with the death of his parents, he inherited a large farm and the care of a younger sister. But one day, hearing the Gospel text, "Go, sell what thou hast, give it to the poor and thou shalt have treasure in heaven," he did so, keeping only enough for their simplest needs. Soon after he again heard the Scriptures read, this time, "Be not solicitous for tomorrow," and he gave away their remaining goods, placed his sister with a group of pious women (the first recorded mention of a convent) and began to live as an ascetic in the manner of various holy men in the vicinity.

Going about among them, he noticed "how gracious was one, how intensely prayerful another . . . of one he observed long vigils, of another the eager love for reading . . . and in all he saw the same reverent love for Christ and mutual affection for one another." He listened carefully to what was read so that he forgot none of it, and later his memory served him in place of books.

Choosing this way of life, not so much as an escape from the world as the straight and narrow road of the Gospels, in time Antony removed himself to the Lybian desert where he dwelt in an abandoned tomb carved out of a mountainside, the scene of the famous temptations. Furious as they were, he battled them more furiously with fastings and prayer, and after a time he "saw the roof open, a ray of light shine through it, and his anguish ceased. 'Where were you?' he challenged the vision, and the answer came, 'I was here, Antony, waiting and watching your struggle. Because you have endured and conquered, I will make your name known throughout the world.' " He was thirty-five.

Even in seclusion his reputation for holiness, as well as the number of his admirers, increased so that he moved still further away to a mountain called Pispir where he lived in an abandoned fort, piling rocks before the door to keep out intruders. There he stayed for almost twenty years until at last his devotees pulled down the rocks and, in response to their pleas, he descended from the mountain to found his first monastery. Even though he was to establish many more such communities, he never stayed with any of them for long, but he visited them from time to time to direct and counsel.

During the persecutions of Maximinus Daza, Antony went to Alexandria to comfort the Christians in prison awaiting their martyrdom. While there, he met Didymus, the blind head of the catechetical school, and bade him not regret too much the loss of his sight, which was shared even with the insects, but rather to rejoice in the inner light by which we see God. While in the city, Greek philosophers came to discuss with Antony, often with more condescension than respect, and went away astonished that the wisdom of this famed solitary was the product of silence and prayer rather than a mastery of texts.

When at last the persecutions ceased, Antony was determined to flee even deeper into the desert. Taking as a companion the monk Macarius, he settled in a spot in the mountains where there was a small grove of date palms and a fresh spring. Even so, his friends found him, but he would see them only after Macarius had separated the true seekers from the merely curious. And this time, in return for his counsel, he asked that they bring him seeds and tools so he might start a garden.

To his monks, astounded that the Emperor Constantine and his sons wrote to Antony asking a remembrance in his prayers, Antony said, "Be not so astounded that the emperor has written to us, but that God has spoken to us—by his Son." And to the emperor he wrote, "Remember daily the judgment to come."

In 399, in a dream of mules kicking at the altars of the church, Antony saw the havoc wrought by the Arian heresy and, at the request of the bishops, he went again to Alexandria to preach that God the Son is not a creature only but of the same substance as the Father. It was during the struggles with the Arians that St. Athanasius, the bishop of Alexandria, seven times exiled, twice took refuge in the desert with Antony and his monks. St. Paul of Thebes was another friend, and legend tells us that when Antony sought him out in the desert, the two men were fed daily by a raven who brought them a loaf of bread; the same bird who for forty years had daily brought the hermit Paul half a loaf.

Another story tells how St. Antony learned in a vision that for all his self-denial, he had not equaled the holiness of a certain poor cobbler in Alexandria. Vexed and astonished, he hurried to the city to ask the cobbler the secret of his sanctity. Surprised, the man told Antony that, on the contrary, he considered himself the worst of sinners and was constantly lamenting to God that all other men were better than he.

Antony of Egypt died, having maintained the same fervor and austerity since his youth. He lived without sickness, his sight was unimpaired, his teeth were worn but not one was loose or missing, and it was always said of him that among any group of monks, he could be identified by the radiant joy of his face.

January 28

Saint Thomas Aquinas
1225–1274

Thomas Aquinas was born in the year 1225 in a fortified castle in Sicily. The youngest son of noble parents, he was sent off at the age of five as a pupil to the
Benedictine abbey at Monte Cassino, probably with the
hope that like other Aquinos before him, he would end up
an abbot. Few glimpses of the young Thomas survive but
one detail is consistently remarked, his preoccupation with
the question: "What is God?" At fourteen, he went to the
University at Naples to study, and here two of the most
important events of his life took place. He read for the
first time the works of Aristotle, and he met Blessed Jordan of Saxony, master general of the Friars Preachers and
successor to St. Dominic.

Jordan was a preacher of such extraordinary eloquence
that he has been called the first of the university chaplains,
and no less a giant than Albert the Great had succumbed
to him. Now, as a student, Thomas Aquinas made the
acquaintance of his religious order and found that it
existed to answer the very question he had asked himself
since childhood. It seemed too good to be true and he
determined to join them.

· 13

Since the Dominicans were considered dangerously radical and his family's Benedictine affiliations could prove to be an obstacle, Thomas's superiors dispatched him to Paris for his studies, but two of his brothers waylaid him on the journey and, although he fought fiercely, they managed to kidnap him and take him to one of the family strongholds. Here he spent a year locked up and, in spite of every attempt to dissuade him, held to his desire to be a Dominican.

There is a story that his brothers, convinced that his loneliness could be preyed upon, sent a girl into his room to seduce him. When Thomas saw her, he seized a burning brand from the fireplace and drove her out (surely screaming) and then with the charred stick drew a cross on the door and fell to his knees. Afterwards he told his closest friend that when he slept, he dreamed of being girded by angels with a cord signifying chastity. In the end, his family had to admit defeat and he set out once more for Paris.

In 1248, Thomas went to Cologne to study with Albert the Great. There he was notable among his fellows only for his gigantic size—six-and-a-half feet tall with a great square cranium set on a thick neck and a barrel of a trunk. He was always quiet, and for his silence and his size the students nicknamed him the Dumb Ox. It is said that Albert, discovering the extraordinary mind at work in this young genius, exclaimed: "You call this lad a dumb ox, but I tell you the whole world is going to hear his bellowing!"

After he was ordained, he returned to Paris where he studied, lectured, taught, and began to adapt the philosophical system of Aristotle to the defense of Christian truth. To propose that reason rather than orthodoxy for its own sake was the proper guide for reexamining the truths of revelation was such an innovation that Thomas was called both genius and radical; his ideas received world acclaim only after the posthumous charge of heresy had been lifted from his *Summa Theologica*.

In this gigantic work, Thomas set forth everything he knew by reason and revelation about God, using the rich resources of the past and his own dazzling insight. He put it all down, he said, because it had so often been said badly, and with such little precision, that students were only fatigued and bored. In its thirty-eight major treatises, more than ten thousand objections are lodged by Thomas against his own teachings—and convincingly refuted. These objections represent a cross section of the history of ideas down to the thirteenth century, from pagan, Greek, and Roman philosophers, from Arabic and Saracen, and from the earliest fathers of the Christian Church.

Strangely enough, he never finished the *Summa*. On the feast of St. Nicholas in 1273, he appeared to be struck by an astonishing change during his celebration of the Mass, and after that he wrote no more. Asked why by his secretary, he answered, "In comparison to the things I have seen, and that have been revealed to me, everything I have written seems straw." He knew only that the answer to his childhood question could never be put down on paper.

There is a legend that Luther burned the *Summa*, together with the papal bull that censured his teachings, in the marketplace at Wittenburg, but a modern scholar (Joseph Pieper) has written that the true story is quite different. "A recent report of that auto-da-fé testifies that there was no one found who was willing to part with his copy." (One might suspect Luther among them.)

What was he like? Pleasing to look at, they said, his skin the deep golden cast characteristic of Sicilians, a man who, in spite of his size, walked with swinging gait and, because of his size, was gaped at from all sides. There is no evidence that he was obese; rather, his secretaries had to remind him to eat. Certainly the tale of the piece cut out of the refectory table to accommodate his girth is apocryphal. He was the typically absent-minded professor lost in his thoughts. One night when he was dining at the palace of the king of France, he startled everyone by striking the table with his fist and exclaiming, "There! That settles the Manichaeans!"

Once he was approached by a brother from another house who did not know him. Thomas was told to accompany him to the city on an errand. He did so, although with some difficulty as the younger brother walked very rapidly. Passers-by stared. What was this? The great Thomas, the most distinguished scholar of Christendom, tagging along behind an unknown friar? Told who it was, the young man was overwhelmed and apologetic. Why had he not protested? But, said Thomas, since God had humbled himself for our sake, ought we not submit to one another for love of him?

He died on March 7, 1274, in a Cistercian monastery in Fossanova, midway in the journey to attend the Council of Lyons. The subprior at Fossanova, who was partially blind, touched Thomas's body and his sight was restored. St. Thomas Aquinas is the patron of students and schools.

January 31

Saint John Bosco
1815–1888

John Bosco was born in a Piedmontese village on the 16th of August, 1815, the youngest son of a peasant farmer and his wife. When he was two, his father died during a time of such terrible poverty that his widow was hard put to set anything at all on the table. But bare as their board might be, Margaret Bosco served her sons such a banquet of stories, lessons, entertainments, and faith as to turn their hardships into the stuff of character, at least for this one son, and his story can hardly be told without including his remarkable mother.

Fairy tales, legends, Bible stories, lives of the saints, catechism, and prayers were her largesse. When she took her sons to the village fairs, the youngest lad watched the jugglers and learned their tricks, mastered ventriloquism, studied the tightrope artists, and acquired skills he would use all his life to win the hearts of hundreds and hundreds of boys.

From the beginning, he had a passion for teaching about Christ. But he also had a temper which would often explode and undo all the good of his lessons. Once in a dream he saw himself rush angrily, shaking his fists, at a crowd of cursing boys until a figure of light said, "You will not win them with blows but with kindness. I will give you a mistress to guide you. . . ." And there was a woman of light, pointing to the boys, now a pack of wild beasts. She said, "This is your field; be humble, strong, courageous."

He conceived the idea of giving shows—juggling, ventriloquy, tightrope dancing. Admission: One rosary. To objections he was adamant: No rosary, no show. On Sundays he led the villagers in prayer and read to them from the Gospel. On winter evenings he visited their homes to tell them stories—but first, a few prayers.

One evening, a mission priest, questioning him, discovered to his surprise that this ten-year-old boy had given his heart to God but didn't know what to do about it. He offered to tutor him and after a year John was ready for school in Castelnuova. Treated contemptuously for his country ways, after one rebuff from a priest, he vowed, "If I am ever a priest, I will never talk to children like that; I will be their friend."

At school in Chieri—where the villagers donated eggs, cheese, butter, and grain to be sold for his tuition—he made up three years' work in one summer, and as the oldest and biggest boy in the class he became a leader. One time he was taking a group of boys to devotions when an acrobat set up his apparatus outside the church. Challenging the man to a contest after Vespers, John suggested a race—and won. A jumping contest? John won. The dancing stick? John had learned that trick at the village fairs, and danced the stick with his hat balanced on top across each finger, his palm, up his arm, shoulder, chin, nose, forehead, and back. The acrobat scaled a great tree beside the church. John did the same and then stood on his hands at the top. The students were hysterical, the acrobat disgusted, John grinning. The loser paid for supper at a nearby inn and promised never to interfere with devotions again.

In the seminary, John had a recurring dream in which he sat in a tailor's room wearing a cassock and sewing patches on old garments. His spiritual director interpreted it as God calling him to work not with new garments, the pure and the innocent, but to patch the soiled and the worn, the weak and the fallen.

John was ordained at twenty-five and went to Turin, where the streets were running with homeless boys from the country in to find work, sleeping anywhere, eating what they could beg or steal, learning all kinds of vices. But they were not easy to befriend. It was weeks before they trusted him enough to respond. Then one Sunday six ragged, dirty, vermin-ridden teenagers showed up—and that was the beginning. More came, and then more, until his work began to be criticized in respectable clerical circles. "Bosco is mad. He should be in a hospital!" Two fellow priests came to take him for a ride one afternoon— their secret destination the local asylum. But John Bosco could read thoughts, and after graciously helping them into the carriage, he slammed the door and instructed the driver, "To the asylum! They are expected!"

He leased a shed in the worst part of the city and with the boys' help made it into a room for work, recreation, study, and chapel. Then, just as things were looking up, he collapsed from exhaustion and pneumonia. But adversity has its own blessings; not a boy was not on his knees, praying, making promises, weeping with contrition, anything, if only God would spare their "Father." And he did. But John now needed help, and his mother came to the close, dirty slum, bringing her own belongings, only to have them stolen or destroyed. She scolded and stormed, yet took the strays in to sleep in her kitchen. Her "goodnight," a short talk about God before bedtime, became a Salesian custom all over the world.

Finally Don Bosco bought the house that went with the shed, kept thirty boys there, fed them—sometimes miraculously—started classes, and in time five hundred boys came. But what was most remarkable was his treatment of the boys. It was a time when severe discipline and harsh punishment were customary, yet Don Bosco never used or allowed such punishment. As much as possible, he eliminated the time and occasion for misbehavior, and required the teachers to love the boys and see them as belonging to God.

The violent anticlericalism in Italy in those days soon picked Don Bosco for a target. After a near beating, he always took a bodyguard of boys when he visted the sick. He was shot at, given poisoned wine, and once a "dying woman" had sons at her bedside armed with clubs. A fracas ensued, the lights went out—and then came Grigio. No one ever knew who Grigio was and Don Bosco never told. He was a great gray dog who appeared when Don Bosco went out at night, attacked ruffians who lay in wait for him, sometimes even refused to let him out the door if danger lay nearby. When at last the vendetta petered out, Grigio disappeared.

In time, Don Bosco called together a special group of boys and formed a company dedicated to Our Lady under the patronage of St. Francis de Sales—thus, Salesians. His mother's death was a grief to him, his poor health a constant suffering, but most painful of all was the discovery of enemies within the church. Jealous of his friendship with Pope Pius IX, clerics intercepted their letters to each other so that each man died wondering why his friend never wrote any more. Add to this the frequent, seemingly diabolical, attacks, and it is a wonder that he remained sweet, good-humored, calm, and agreeable.

By the end of his life he had established houses for boys all over Europe and organized a community of women to staff houses for homeless girls. He had lost the sight of one eye, could walk only with a cane, and finally at seventy-three, he was paralyzed. His weeping sons surrounded his bed and prayed for his life but he refused to join them. It was time to see God—and he did, on January 31, 1888.

Saint Brigid of Ireland
c. 453

S t. Brigid of Ireland was born around the year 453, probably near Kildare, the daughter of a Christian bondwoman, Brocessa, and a minor pagan king, Dubthac (pronounced Duffack—the equivalent of Duffy). Before Brigid's birth her mother was sold to a druid; and because the offspring of such a union was the property of the original owner, when the girl was old enough she was returned to her father's household and assumed her mother's tasks—grinding the corn, washing the feet of guests, and tending the sheep, pigs, and cows.

If some of the stories of Brigid tax credulity, her vision of Christ in the needy was never disputed and was surely harder to live with than any of the miracles, trying not only the patience of everyone who knew her but later the very forbearance of some of her nuns.

Half slave and half princess, Brigid was submissive and obedient until circumstances required a regal gesture, and that she always made—"To honor Christ," she said, "for Christ is in the body of every poor man." She gave bacon for the guests to a stray dog and there was still enough bacon; every day she gave butter to the poor and there was always butter. Did a poor man come to beg as she was tending sheep? Like as not, she gave him a sheep.

So profligate was her giving that her father, in anger, decided to sell Brigid to the king of Leinster, a Christian chief said to have been baptized by St. Patrick. Driving her to the king's fortress in his chariot, he left her to wait outside while he angrily explained his errand to the king. Brigid, in the meantime, was approached by a leper who asked an alms for the love of God. Without anything of her own to give him, Brigid handed over her father's great battle sword, which had been left in her keeping in the chariot. Furious, her father dragged her before the king and berated the folly of giving such a priceless possession to a begger. But when the king questioned her, Brigid answered simply that a priceless gift was never unsuitable as a gift to God. To his credit, the king rebuked Dubthac: "Leave her alone, for her merit before God is greater than ours." And she was taken home. True or invented—and it could well be true—it is a tale that perfectly illustrates Brigid's understanding of Christian freedom. She simply saw with the vision of the Gospels.

She asked her father's permission to visit her mother, and when it was denied she went all the same, convinced that it was right and just. When she discovered her mother broken in health, Brigid herself took on the task of caring for twelve cows, the milking, the butter-making, and—as one might expect—presumed the freedom to give what was needed to the poor. The druid, hearing of her benefi- cence, visited her with his wife and brought a large hamper which they demanded be filled with butter. There was not enough, as they well knew, but to their surprise Brigid filled it. In response the awed master gave her the herd of cows. She refused the gift but asked instead for her mother's freedom, which was granted.

Upon returning to her father, Brigid discovered his plans for her marriage, but she was determined that she would belong only to Christ. Out of consideration for the bridegroom-to-be (a poet—and poets were ranked among the mighty in those days), she found him another and more suitable wife and then set out in search of other Christian women like herself who were vowed to the single life. Many such, both bondwomen and free, endured the scorn of their families at home as they divided their time between chores, prayer, and works of mercy. Brigid determined to form a community of women like the communities of monks already established by St. Patrick before her. Eventually, she and seven companions made their vows before St. Mel, a nephew of St. Patrick, and established the first of her foundations. By the end of her life, she had brought thirteen thousand women from the fortresses of chieftans and the hovels of slavery to a new life as free nuns living in monasteries and dedicated to Christ.

Tradition says that Brigid was beautiful, a lover of gaiety, a bountiful hostess, with an ear for music and good conversation. As a nun she dressed in white, but is said to have worn a purple-red cloak. Far from living the enclosed life, she traveled indefatigably across the land and back, accompanied in her chariot by two nuns and driven by a priest who sat on a small seat in front.

Kildare, the greatest of her foundations, was enclosed by great stone and earthen walls, within which was the monastic settlement. Built of stone with thatched roofs, artisans' dwellings and workshops lined the main pathway—smithy, carpenter shop, refectory, kitchen, guest chambers, library, church, and community cells. Set in fields of green dotted with grazing herds, these settlements were a hive of industry and out of them came some of the most beautiful craftsmanship in the history of Christendom. This great monastery produced quantities of beautiful bells, crosiers, chalices, patens, bookrests, and the most spectacular work of them all, the Book of Kildare, which is said now by some scholars to be, possibly, the Book of Kells.

Yet for all her fame and wisdom and learning, Brigid's setting was the country life, and until the end she could be found milking cows and making butter, rounds of cheese, and tubs of home-brewed ale. When St. Brendan went finally to meet her, Brigid came from her sheep to welcome him and, legend tells us, hung her cloak, wet with rain, on the rays of the sun. Brendan hung his there also, but his fell down.

There are endless and charming legends of St. Brigid. She saved a man condemned to die for accidentally killing the pet fox of her old friend, the king of Leinster. By calling another fox from the wood and teaching it to do tricks, she calmed the king and saved the man's life.

It was said that the Mother of God, sorely tried by crowds marveling at her beauty and following her wherever she went, asked Brigid, "Can you help me?" And she did, bringing out a great field rake whose metal teeth flashed like candles so that the distracted crowd stayed to watch. Asked by Mary what reward she would have, Brigid answered, "Put my day before your own." That is why, tradition holds, St. Brigid's day is on the first of February and Our Lady's Feast of the Purification on the second. For centuries, February first was the day St. Brigid's crosses of woven straw were put over the doors, and housekeepers repeated a rhyme which bids them bring out a portion of butter to divide among the working boys.

Brigid of Ireland is a joyful, invigorating saint, who comes to us wiping her hands on her apron, her face shining with welcome, her heart filled with the Lord, her hand always out to the poor. More than anything else, she radiates the goodness, the wholeness, the attractiveness of the Christian life as revealed by a loving, faith-filled, free Christian woman.

February 6

The Nagasaki Martyrs (St. Paul Miki and Companions)
Died 1597

The twenty-six Nagasaki martyrs were the first to be canonized of all those who died for their faith in Japan's short-lived Christian century. Even the additional 205 beatified martyrs account for only a fraction of the thousands of Japanese Christians who were robbed, driven from their homes, tried, sent to prison, tortured for their faith, and executed. They could have saved themselves by recanting. Many did, but many more only pretended to while remaining secretly faithful. Their descendents cling to what they know of Christianity to this very day.

Some of their stories have been documented and books have been written about some of their missionaries. But one can only know the others by studying the art of the period, the paintings of common folk to be found on fans and scrolls, in albums, and on the great folding screens. There, in little vignettes of village life showing the carpenter, the potter, the shopkeeper, the weaver, the families and children, one can see them in their own setting— a land of exquisite beauty where delicacy of manners could exist side by side with horrifying cruelty. These were the kind of people whose names, together with the missionaries', appear on the lists of the martyrs of Japan.

The sixteenth century was one of the most turbulent in

Japanese history. The emperor's powers were relegated to the *shogun,* a commander-in-chief who ruled over the *diamyos,* feudal lords who in turn ruled their fiefs with the aid of their knights, the *samurai.* By the time St. Francis Xavier arrived in 1549, an all-powerful *daimyo,* Nobunaga, controlled most of Japan and gave the first Jesuit missionaries permission to preach and build churches. At the death of Nobunaga, control was seized by a military genius named Hideyoshi who unified the country under a central government and, for a while, continued to favor the missionaries—for where the Fathers were, the trading vessels came. Thus converts multiplied, sometimes by the thousands, as whole fiefs were baptized upon the conversion of their respective lords.

Hideyoshi's change of heart, fed by his growing fear of the unity of the Christian lords, was probably touched off by the imprudent efforts of the Jesuit superior to bring Spanish soldiers to secure the Christian position on the island of Kyushu. When Father Coelho sailed to Hakata on a well-armed ship for an audience with Hideyoshi, the ruler asked to see the ship and hinted that it be given to him. Ignoring the advice of the alarmed Christian lords, Coelho refused and, inevitably, Hideyoshi became irritated.

At the same time, a large Portuguese ship which had arrived at Hirado was ordered by Hideyoshi to proceed to Hakata. Fearful of the shallow waters, the captain came to explain why he could not obey. Although Hideyoshi seemed to accept his explanation, that night he turned persecutor. Already resentful, now suspicious and half drunk with Coelho's Portuguese wine, he ordered all missionaries out of Japan in twenty days.

After some burning of churches and threats of death, things remained as before, except that the fathers, to be less conspicuous, substituted *kimonos* for their religious garb and proceeded with their work more cautiously.

But distrust was growing. European globes and world maps were known in Japan, and the Spanish conquests had begun to arouse fears. When, in October of 1596, the Spanish ship *San Felipe,* bound for Mexico, was wrecked off the port of Urado, the Japanese confiscated her cargo. Hideyoshi, reminded by the Franciscan superior that he had granted safe passage to Spanish ships in Japan, had to find a pretext for the seizure. He claimed that the ship was armed and the priests aboard might be spies.

Unfortunately, at Urado the pilot of the *San Felipe,* meaning only to impress the Japanese into releasing his ship, was cleverly tricked into boasting of the power of the Spanish king. Pointing to the Spanish colonies on the map of the world, he admitted that when establishing trade with new lands the Spanish always brought missionaries first—and Hideyoshi's worse suspicions were confirmed. The ship was seized and the passengers commanded to return to Manila. One Franciscan, Felip de Jesus de las Casas, a Mexican cleric on his way home for ordination, was able to make his way to the Franciscan priory in Miako (Kyoto). There he was seized and, with the others, condemned to death. He was the first North American-born saint to be canonized.

On December 8 the friars in Miako were arrested and twenty-four men were condemned. Among them were the Franciscans' superior in Japan, Father Pedro Bautista, Fathers Martin Aguirre and Francisco Blanco; Brothers Francisco de San Miguel and Gonzalo Garcia. The latter, born in India, is said by some to have been Portuguese, by others to have had Indian parents who took Portuguese names at baptism. If the latter is true, he is the first canonized saint from India. Three Japanese Jesuits were arrested by mistake (the order applied only to Franciscans)—Brother Paul Miki, a brilliant preacher; and two Jesuit candidates, acolyte John Soan de Goto and catechist Diogo Kisai.

Together with the religious, there were seventeen Japanese laymen: Leo Karasumuru, chief lay preacher for the Franciscans; Paul Ibaraki, brother to Leo; Louis Ibaraki (age 10), acolyte and nephew of Leo and Paul; Paul Suzuki, preacher; Thomas Dangi, a former merchant who had turned his house into a hospice for the poor; Anthony (age 13), acolyte; Gabriel (age 19), acolyte, a handsome young man of noble birth whose conversion had been a scandal in court circles; Bonaventura, an acolyte and former *bonze* (Buddhist priest); Francis, a doctor and former *samurai;* Thomas, his son (age 16), an acolyte, the one who had guided Felipe de Jesus to Miako; and Joshim Sakakibara, a cook for the Franciscans in Osaka. One Matthias was absent, but the friars' cook, also named Matthias, insisted upon taking his place.

Thrown into a single prison cell, they heard Hideyoshi's first sentence: to have their ears and noses cut off in the public square and to be paraded through the streets. The sentence was reduced to cutting off a part of one ear, and as they were drawn through the streets in ox carts, Father Bautista explained to the people why they were glad to suffer for their Lord.

On January 4 they left Miako on horseback, sitting cross-legged on wooden saddles. Their final sentence was to be crucified in Nagasaki, fastened to crosses with iron bands at wrists, ankles, and throat, the body resting on a saddle piece, and death coming by two lance thrusts diagonally through the torso. Behind them followed Francisco Falename, a Japanese carpenter who had vowed to stay with them in their need.

They were led through cities, towns, and villages, sometimes walking, sometimes on horseback. Following the coast, they walked barefoot through slush and snow, crossed icy streams, and climbed mountain trails. Those who collapsed were stuffed into bamboo litters. Weak with dysentery and malnutrition, they sang and recited the rosary. They consoled the weeping Christians along the way and were stoned by the pagans. The faithful carpenter was finally added to their number, as was Pedro Sukejiroo, another helper who joined them on the journey.

At Karatsu, a humanitarian custodian allowed them to go with hands unbound, and granted their request to be allowed to die on Friday and to receive Holy Communion before they died. He also offered the boys their freedom, but they refused. In sight of Nagasaki, they ended their journey on foot in obedience to their rule. Sick, depressed, stumbling, their hearts lifted at the sight of two Jesuits bringing them the Eucharist—only to see them turned away. Their benefactor had decided the risk was too great. But the two Jesuit candidates were allowed to make their vows and all were permitted to go to confession. Commander Lanchedo of the *San Felipe,* who had been trying to catch up to them and offer ransom, arrived at last but his request was refused.

February 5 was a Wednesday, bright, cold, with a light sifting of snow over the city. They were taken to the Hill of Wheat where hundreds of weeping Japanese Christians had defied orders and flocked to meet them with gifts of food and wine, and with pleas for blessings and relics. The prisoners tasted the food for courtesy's sake and gave away their rosaries, medals, and crosses.

Twenty-six crosses awaited them, each bearing a man's name. The boys, seeing three small crosses, ran to them, while the others walked down the line searching for their names. Paul Miki called to the crowd that martyrdom was not a cause for sorrow but for jubilation. They were fastened to the crosses, the lances were raised—and one by one they died. In the harbor, from the deck of the Portuguese carrack moored there, the survivors of the *San Felipe* watched.

Today less than one percent of Japan is Christian, and the Church has still to find words and concepts which can speak to a culture so far from the Hellenism which produced the dominant imagery and thought forms of the Christian West. But what is a problem for Japan is now a problem for the West also. Perhaps, if the blood of the martyrs is the seed of the church, the Japanese martyrs will serve not only to discover a way of revealing Christ to their own ancient culture in the East, but also to the people who live now in the new technological culture of the West.

February 10

Saint Scholastica
c. 480–c. 543

According to tradition, St. Scholastica and St. Benedict were twins, and as a little girl Scholastica is said to have consecrated herself wholly to God. It is not known whether she lived at home or with a community of pious women, but after her brother moved to Monte Cassino, she founded a convent about five miles to the south of Benedict's monastery. St. Gregory says in his *Dialogues* (two chapters of which are the only source of information on Scholastica) that Benedict ruled nuns as well as monks, and it is likely that Scholastica was an abbess under his direction.

Scholastica used to visit Benedict once a year, and since she was not allowed to enter his monastery, Benedict would go with some of his monks to meet her at a house a little way off. They spent their time praying together and talking about the spiritual life. In the story of their last visit, Gregory tells that they spoke of the things of God all day long, ate their supper together, and continued their conversation far into the night. Then Scholastica, seeing that it was time for her brother to leave, said, "Please, do not leave me tonight, my brother. Let us keep on talking about the joys of heaven until morning."

"What are you saying, my sister?" Benedict replied. "You know I cannot stay away from the monastery." At Benedict's refusal, Scholastica folded her hands on the table and rested her head on them in prayer. It was late, and a beautiful night, the sky was clear and without a trace of a cloud. But when she looked up again, there was a sudden burst of lightning and thunder, accompanied by such a downpour that Benedict and his companions were not able to set foot outside the door.

Realizing that he could not return to the monastery, Benedict rebuked his sister. "God forgive you, sister!" he said. "What have you done!" Scholastica replied simply, "When I appealed to you, you would not listen to me. So I turned to my God and he heard my prayer. Leave me here now, if you can, and go back to your monastery."

Of course he could not. He had no choice but to stay in spite of his unwillingness. And once he was over his annoyance, Benedict and Scholastica talked until dawn about the life of the soul.

The next morning, Scholastica returned to her convent and Benedict to his monastery. Three days later, as he stood at his window looking up toward the sky, Benedict saw his sister's soul, in the form of a dove, leaving her body and entering the court of heaven. Joyful, he sang a hymn of praise in thanks to God and told his brother monks of her death, sending them to bring her body to the monastery. It was buried in the tomb which he had long before prepared for the two of them.

It is a nice little story, at first glance rather trivial and unimportant, until we consider that of all our possessions, the one most prized by those who need us is our loving presence. Even St. Benedict had allowed himself to put rules and regulations before the need of his sister, who simply wanted him to talk with her.

As a consequence of this tale, St. Scholastica is invoked against storms, but she might better be the patron saint of relationships, a saint to help us discern whether it is more important to keep our schedules tidy or to be available to people when they need us.

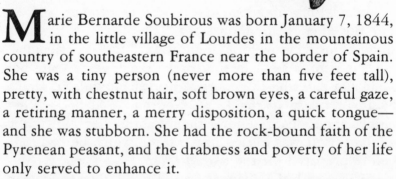

February 11

Our Lady of Lourdes

April 16

and Saint Bernadette Soubirous
1844–1879

Marie Bernarde Soubirous was born January 7, 1844, in the little village of Lourdes in the mountainous country of southeastern France near the border of Spain. She was a tiny person (never more than five feet tall), pretty, with chestnut hair, soft brown eyes, a careful gaze, a retiring manner, a merry disposition, a quick tongue— and she was stubborn. She had the rock-bound faith of the Pyrenean peasant, and the drabness and poverty of her life only served to enhance it.

Her parents were good but impractical people and by the time she was ten they had lost their livelihood as millers and were reduced to living in a wretched hovel called "the dungeon" because it once was a jail. Unfit for prisoners, it had become a stable. Unfit for beasts, it was abandoned until the destitute Soubirouses made it their home. There, in spite of vermin and a manure heap in the yard, the mother kept them meticulously tidy and clean, and with odd jobs the father kept them fed—but just barely.

Bernadette was the eldest and because she suffered from asthma, she did not attend school. She did not mind staying at home to help except that it prevented her from making her First Communion because she could not read or write. To remedy this, at thirteen she went to live with the Lagües family in Bartrés in order to take instructions. Things went well until the local curé went off to be a monk and the Lagües family unfairly put her to tending their sheep. She was reduced to studying with the testy Mme. Lagües, who often would throw the book down and cry, "You dullard, you will never learn anything!" The catechism was in French and Bernadette knew only the local dialect. So early one morning she finally marched herself back home to enter school along with the beginners. She was fourteen years old when at last she began to prepare for her First Communion.

On that famous February 11th in 1858, she was taking off her woolen stockings so she could wade across a shallow river after her sister and a friend to search for firewood. Suddenly she heard a wind, looked up and saw, across the river in a niche in the rock, a lovely girl in white with a pearly rosary hanging from her arm, a radiance about her head, and two yellow roses at the toes of her bare feet.

Frightened, Bernadette reached for her rosary and knelt there praying, watching the girl count her own beads but move her lips only for the *Gloria.* "She was wearing a white dress reaching down to her feet . . . gathered very high at the neck by a hem from which hung a white cord. A white veil covered her head and came down over her shoulders and arms almost to the bottom of her dress. The sash of the dress was blue and hung down below her knees. . . . She was alive, very young, and surrounded by light." Her face was oval and "of incomparable grace," her eyes were blue, and her voice—"Oh, so sweet!"

The vision lasted for the time it took to say a rosary. Then the girls caught sight of Bernadette, motionless and white, and for a moment they thought she was dead. Frightened, they threw two small stones at her and suddenly she came to herself again. On the way home, she told them what she had seen, and in no time her mother was scolding her for making up stories. But she was allowed to go again on condition that next time she sprinkle the figure with holy water and say, "If you are from God, then stay!" She did, and the girl smiled and stayed. Once more Bernadette was in ecstasy until the frightened girls called a passer-by to drag her away.

In no time, the town began to get excited. Determined to keep her home to avoid trouble, her parents forbade her to go to the grotto again. Then two respectable village ladies, convinced that this was the shade of a recently deceased Child of Mary, offered to accompany her—but early in the morning before dawn to avoid notice. They gave Bernadette paper and pen and told her to ask the lady to write her name. When she did the lady refused, this time laughing. Then she asked Bernadette to come to the grotto for a fortnight and her reply was, "I will, if my parents will let me," which they did, although with some uneasiness.

By the end of the fortnight, she was the talk of the region. Thousands of people knew about the vision, hundreds were coming to see her, and the opinions raged. The pious were convinced that the lady was the Blessed Virgin, the impious that Bernadette was a cataleptic child who belonged in a mental hospital, and that the affair was a trick of the Soubirouses to get money. Bernadette was interrogated by the mayor, the police, the local monseigneur, and was accused of lying, chicanery, and exhibitionism. No one was able to trick her into contradicting her story or frighten her into abandoning it, in spite of threats to send her to jail, to the insane asylum, or to hell and eternal damnation.

Questioned about scratching in the dirt and drinking the muddy water (the day before the Lourdes spring began to flow), and for eating a bit of herb and grass, she was told "The Blessed Virgin wouldn't ask you to eat grass! People don't eat grass, animals do!" She replied crisply, "Oh yes, people do. Only they put oil and vinegar on it and call it salad."

Monseigneur Peyramale, the local pastor, consistently ignored the affair until finally Bernadette came to him with a message. "The lady wants a chapel," she said. In a fury he shouted at her, "Get her to tell you her name! Get her to make the roses bloom!" The sisters at the hospice where she went to school, just as skeptical, snapped, "Well, if it is the Blessed Virgin, get her to teach you your catechism!"

Twice the lady did not appear, and Bernadette cried as though her heart would break. When she was there again, she told three secrets to Bernadette and taught her a prayer for herself alone. She bade her to do penance for sinners, and promised that although she would not be happy in this life, she would be in heaven. But she did not tell her name. The apparitions ceased when the fortnight was over.

Several weeks later on the morning of March 25th, the Feast of the Annunciation, Bernadette heard an inner command to go to the grotto. "She [the lady] was there, tranquil and smiling and watching the crowd just as a fond mother watches her children." Bernadette knelt, apologized for being late, told the lady she loved her, and began to say her beads. The lady came nearer, almost tête-à-tête, and Bernadette asked, "Madame, will you be so kind as to tell me who you are?" The lady bowed and smiled, unclasped her hands, brought them down to her sides (as they appear on the Miraculous Medal), crossed them again, pressed them to her breast, and said: "I am the Immaculate Conception." And she disappeared.

It was only four years since the dogma of the Immaculate Conception had been proclaimed by Pius IX, and Bernadette did not even know what it was. She kept repeating the words aloud to herself all the way to the rectory door and when he opened it, she told Monseigneur Peyramale. He said, "I was so amazed that I felt myself stagger and I was on the point of falling." He barked at her, "Do you know what it means?" and she replied, "No, Monsieur le Curé."

Eventually Bernadette entered the novitiate of the Sisters of Charity of Never, who had taught her at the hospice. "I am like a broom that one sweeps with, and when the task is finished, it is put behind the door," she said to her classmates, rejoicing that at last she could escape the publicity, the crowds gazing at her, the endless summons to the parlor to be inspected. But it did not cease, nor the collecting of "relics"—snips of her hair, her sewing, scraps of her handwriting. Once she gave a few sugared almonds to some children and within minutes, the adults had taken them away.

After at first being warmly welcomed by the Mother General and the Mistress of Novices, her penance for sinners began in earnest as these two women—in the spirit of keeping her humble, they said—treated her with unbelievable coldness and disdain. One night as she lay deathly ill, the bishop was called so that she could make her pro-

fession of vows and receive the veil. Her superiors wanted
to make sure that if she died, it would be as a Sister of
Charity of Nevers. Immediately, she began to revive. The
Mother General, angry, said, "If you do not die by morning, I will take this veil from you!" Once she confided to
another sister, concerning the Mistress of Novices, "How
I fear her!" Even after Bernadette's death, this woman who
had now become Mother General still could not accept
such a divine *faux pas*. "I still don't understand why the
Blessed Virgin appeared to Bernadette. There are so many
others so refined, so well-bred. . . ." Perhaps Bernadette
did owe something to those two women for being the
instruments of her sanctification—although surely love
demands more.

She suffered ghastly ill health with rarely a day without
pain. The tuberculosis of the bone which was wasting her
produced a horrendous tumor on one knee so large that
her leg had to be kept outside the bed covers. The damp-
ness and miasma of "the dungeon," the poverty, the insuf-
ficient food, the asthma were taking their toll. It all tallied
in an endless prayer of penance and she bore it superbly,
cutting away inch by inch at faults she was sure she possessed, enlarging her generosity day by day. She complained that stories of the virtues of the saints were no
help to her, that she wanted to know how they overcame
their faults.

In periods of reasonably good health she was infirmarian, even though on her profession day the Mother General told the bishop, "I don't know what we will do with
her. She is good for nothing." She became a perfect religious. She never referred to her experience in the grotto
unless she was bade to, revealing it only when she
prayed—and they watched to see that look creep over her
face, to see her astonishingly majestic Sign of the Cross, to
hear her say the *Hail Mary*. She taught them how to use

suffering, and in the end, when she was completely bed-ridden, she replied to a visitor who asked her what she was doing in bed all the time, "I am doing my job." "And what is your job, you lazy little thing?" "Being ill."

By the time Bernadette died, Lourdes was a world-famous shrine, approved by the Holy See and frequented by hundreds and thousands of people who invoked Mary under the title of Our Lady of Lourdes. There were cures of wracked and deformed bodies, troubled hearts and souls. She never saw the grotto again, and finally ceased wishing that she could. Her work was to love, to pray, to remain hidden, and to wait for the day when she would see her beloved Lord and her beautiful Lady face to face. Death came after unspeakable suffering on April 16, 1879, at the age of thirty-five. She was canonized by Pius XI on December 8, 1933, the feast of the Immaculate Conception—this little nobody.

March 7

Saint Perpetua and Saint Felicity
Died 203

The story of Sts. Perpetua and Felicity is told in a diary which Perpetua kept until the day they died and which, fortunately, a friend finished after she was forced to leave off. It is one of the oldest authentic documents of the early Church.

Perpetua was twenty-two at the time of the martyrdom in 203, wellborn, married, and the mother of a tiny son still at her breast. Felicity, an expectant mother, was her slave. They were among five catechumens arrested and imprisoned as a warning to the other Christians in Carthage. Tormented by her father, a pagan who wanted her to apostatize, terrified by the darkness and heat of the dungeon where they were imprisoned, Perpetua's greatest suffering nevertheless was for her baby who was still with her. But, she wrote, baptism drove away her fears and with the coming of the Holy Spirit, she was at peace, the prison became to her as a palace, and in visions she learned the manner of their marytrdom and the delight that awaited them in heaven.

For Felicity, the greatest fear was that her baby would not be born in time for her to die with her companions, for there was a law which forbade throwing even a Christian woman to the wild beasts if she was with child. Three days before they were to go to the arena, they prayed together for the birth of her child and no sooner were their prayers finished than her labor began. She gave birth to a little girl who afterwards was adopted by her sister.

Brought to the scene of their marytrdom, Perpetua astounded the onlookers "with the spirit in her eyes," and Felicity beside her rejoiced "to come from the midwife to the gladiator, to wash after her travail in a second baptism." They were told to put on the garments of pagan priestesses, but they refused and were stripped naked, covered with nets, and sent to face assault by a maddened cow, chosen as an insult to their motherhood. Strangely, the audience, though screaming for blood, was touched by the sight of these two so young and valiant and "the people shuddered."

Called back, Perpetua and Felicity were clothed in loose robes and returned to the arena. Perpetua was thrown into the arena first, her garment was rent and her thigh gored. Regaining her feet, she gathered her tunic over her thigh "so in suffering she would not appear immodest." Looking about she found her fallen hair ornament and repinned her hair, "lest one soon to be a martyr seem to grieve in her glory." She helped Felicity to her feet and the two stood together and awaited still another attack, but the mob cried out, "Enough!" and they were saved for the gladiator's sword. Catching sight of her brother, Perpetua cried out, "Stand fast in the faith and love one another; and do not let our sufferings be a stumbling block to you."

Again the people clamored for their execution and after giving each other the kiss of peace, they were killed by the gladiators. Felicity died first, then Perpetua—but only after a nervous swordsman had struck her once and failed. The second time she guided his sword with her own hands.

One hundred and fifty years before, Paul had written to the Galatians: ". . . gone is the distinction between Jew and Greek, slave and free man, male and female—you are all one in Christ Jesus!" Today he would have added "white and black." Perpetua was white, Felicity was black.

March 9
Saint Frances of Rome
1384–1440

St. Frances of Rome was born of a wealthy noble family in the Trastevere district of Rome in 1384, at the beginning of the Great Schism of the West, the forty years during which two, even three popes simultaneously claimed primacy and noble families like her own were safe or in danger depending upon which papal party held sway.

She was raised in luxury but the devotion of her mother led the little girl to a love for prayer and a deep concern for the poor; at ten she decided to become a nun. Her family had other plans, however, and educated her to become the mistress of a noble household. When she was eleven they announced her betrothal to a young nobleman, Lorenzo Ponziano. Although she wept and pleaded, the marriage was much more to her family's advantage and took place.

At thirteen she went to live with Lorenzo's family, who were delighted to have such a noble and pious beauty as the bride of their young heir. Only when she was alone did she surrender to melancholy until eventually her equally young sister-in-law, Vanozza, discovered the reason and confided that she too would have preferred the religious life. Together the two girls consoled each other and vowed that they would thereafter serve the Lord as faithfully in marriage.

In order to please Lorenzo, Frances wore his family jewels and dressed in the silks and velvets he admired, but under them she wore a hair shirt. And when she and Vanozza went abroad to care for the poor, they dressed in plain green stuff with simple veils. It was not long before Lorenzo's relatives discovered his bride's penchant for the unfortunate (a service not admired among the rich at the time), and she became the object of their derision. However, to his credit Lorenzo permitted no one to speak ill of her, for Lorenzo, bless his heart, was a man in love.

Recovering from a near fatal illness, Frances simplified her life still further and increased her austerities, although her confessor would not permit either young woman to set aside the dress of their rank. Inevitably the two began to acquire a reputation for holiness. Not only did some of the fashionable ladies of Rome begin to change their lives but the servants, whom she treated more like brothers and sisters than hirelings, did their work more cheerfully and attended church more often.

Nevertheless, Frances was convinced that family duties took precedence over the service of God and prayer. "It is laudable in a married woman to be devout but she must never forget that she has a household to care for, and sometimes she must leave God at the altar to find him in her housekeeping." One charming story tells that she was reading the Psalter one day when Lorenzo called her three different times to come to his assistance. Each time she put the book down immediately and went to him. Returning the fourth time, she found the words on the page written in gold.

Now violent temptations assaulted her, enticing and

hideous visions, sometimes physical blows. She became aware also of the presence of her guardian angel who on one occasion rebuked a fault by giving her a resounding slap. In addition, her mother-in-law protested to both sons that the two young women were neglecting their duties as hostesses and damaging the reputation of the Ponziano family, until Lorenzo and Paulo told their mother lovingly but firmly to mind her own affairs.

At sixteen Frances bore her first child, Giovanni Baptista. Although it was not the custom for ladies of wealth to nurse their children, she insisted upon it and that she personally attend to the formation of his early years, a notion foreign to the rich even up to the present century. Upon the death of her mother-in-law, Frances became mistress of the household, and when flood, famine, and pestilence struck Rome, she and the servants dispensed charity so generously that her outraged father-in-law finally took the keys. But when he saw the contents of an empty corn bin and an empty wine barrel replenished after her prayer, he yielded, saying: "My dear, you have found the secret of real happiness—unstinting charity and a love that increases in proportion as it is shared." He gave her the freedom of his wealth, and Lorenzo of his, and now at last with the conversion of her husband to the service of the poor, she received permission to adopt simpler dress and to sell her jewels and elaborate gowns.

Two more children—a son, Evangelista, and a daughter, Agnes—were born, and in 1409 Rome and its environs were further devastated by war. Lands were burned, herds slaughtered, noble houses reduced to ruins, the poor made homeless. Lorenzo was kidnaped and held hostage until Baptista should be delivered as ransom. Distraught, Frances prayed, consulted her confessor, and was directed to deliver the child, and to trust as Abraham had trusted. It is said that when the child was delivered and Lorenzo

freed, the horse on which the boy was to be taken away
would not move. His superstitious captor finally sent him
back to his family.

Paulo was kidnaped and exiled; Lorenzo was smuggled
out of the city to escape a similar fate; Baptista was captured, escaped, and joined his father; and Frances, Vanozza, and the children, poor at last like the people they
served, found shelter in a corner of the palace. There
Evangelista died. The Tiber overflowed, bringing plague
to Rome, and once again the two women went to help the
sick and the dying. Frances drove a wagon in which she
collected the abandoned dead for burial, scoured the city
for herbs, for beetles for potions and leeches for bleeding,
gathered wood, and set up a soup kitchen. When they ran
out of food, she and Vanozza went begging. Numerous
stories are told of Frances's gift of healing.

At this time in a vision, 'Lista, accompanied by an archangel, told her of the approaching death of Agnes. The
angel, who Frances described as "the size of an eight-
year-old child," was to stay with her for twenty-three
years, walking beside her at all times except when she
committed a fault, when he faded from sight.

The papacy was finally stabilized, the Ponzianis regained
their properties, and at last Baptista and Lorenzo, now
broken in health, returned. Overjoyed to be with his faithful wife again, Lorenzo released her from all marital obli-
gations except that they dwell together, and finally she was
able to realize her dream of a congregation of women who
would remain in their homes but dedicate their lives to
serving the poor. Once more she met with scorn and
ridicule from Baptista's beautiful but violent tempered
bride, but when the young woman fell ill Frances nursed
her so tenderly that she was quite converted. Later she
kept a priceless journal of her mother-in-law's life.

In time, the members of Frances's foundation started

living in community as the Oblates of Tor de Specchi, and when Lorenzo died she joined them. One evening in 1440 as she was returning from a visit to Baptista, her confessor met her and, shocked at her gaunt and fragile appearance, sent her back. She lived for seven days in her son's home and on the evening of March 9, her face shining, she said: "The angel is beckoning me to follow him." When she died, her body was removed to Santa Maria Nuova for burial and ever since it has been known as the Church of Santa Francesca Romana. Understandably, she is a patroness of Rome.

But she is a patroness of many others also—wives and mothers, the concerned wealthy who wish to serve the poor, the innocent victims of war and poverty, and of that increasing number of men and women who are drawn to pastoral ministry. Juggling the demands of family life and the call to serve her neighbor, she worked and prayed and improvised in season and out, this charming and delightful lady who walked in the company of her guardian angel and became, to all the city of Rome, its guardian angel.

March 17

Saint Patrick
c. 389–c. 461

S t. Patrick says in his *Confession* that he was the son of a
Roman deacon and municipal officer named Calpur-
nius, the grandson of Potitus, a Christian priest, and was
born in Britain (or perhaps Brittany, the birthplace of his
mother). His early education ended at fifteen, a fact that
embarrassed him all his life, and at sixteen he wrote that he
"knew not the true God," meaning that he paid little attention to religion. Shortly thereafter he and a number of
other Christians were kidnaped and taken to be slaves
among the pagan raiders in Ireland.

There he spent six years pasturing flocks, enduring extreme hardships, and there he began to pray again. "The
love and fear of God more and more inflamed my heart;
my faith enlarged, my spirit grew . . . . I said a hundred
prayers by day and almost as many by night. I arose before
day in the snow, in the frost, and the rain, yet I received no
harm . . . for then the spirit of God was within me."

In a dream he heard a voice say he was soon to be free,
and he escaped and ran two hundred miles to the sea. At
first he was refused passage on a ship home but in answer

to his silent prayer, the sailors called him back and he embarked. After three days' sailing, they reached land and traveled for twenty-eight days on foot through unknown country until their provisions ran out. When the shipmaster asked him derisively how the great Lord he worshiped could leave them in such peril, Patrick replied that if they would turn to him, he *would* provide. Shortly after, a herd of wild pigs crossed their path. They killed many, ate their fill, resuscitated their dogs, and offered thanks. At length they reached habitation and Patrick was restored to his family. He was twenty-three.

But now during the night he heard voices calling him back to Ireland: "We beg you, holy youth, to come and walk among us again." To answer this call, he left his family, resumed his education, studied for the priesthood (with his uncle, St. Martin of Tours), and was ordained. In 432, St. Germanus consecrated him bishop and sent him to Ireland to replace Bishop Palladium who had died there.

The most famous story about Patrick tells of his journey to Tara, the court of High King Laoghaire. On the eve of Easter, Patrick and his party encamped at Slaine in sight of Tara, and there Patrick lighted the Easter fire which was visible at the king's court. It was the night of a sacred druidic festival and it was a gross violation of royal orders that any fire should be lighted before the court druids should light their sacred fire. The astonished king, seeing Patrick's blaze in the distance, was filled with wrath. Demanding to know who had done this, the druids are said to have answered that it was the fulfillment of an ancient prophecy, that someone had come to Eirinn to supersede the king's rule and their own. "Unless yonder fire be extinguished this very night, it shall never more be extinguished in Eirinn. It will outshine all fires that we light, and he who lit it will conquer us all."

The king demanded that the transgressor be brought
before him. Patrick's camp was raided and he and his companions ordered to march to Tara. A legend tells us that on
Easter morning the missionaries walked in procession toward the king's court, chanting the sacred *Lorica* or Deer's
Cry—in later years called St. Patrick's Breastplate. As the
minions of the druids lay in ambush to intercept and kill
them, they saw, not Patrick and his men but a gentle doe
followed by twenty fawns.

At the court, the king, his queen, and his courtiers were
sitting silently in state, his warriors in a great circle, their
shields against their chins. All were bade by the king to
show the strangers no mark of respect. But so noble was
Patrick's bearing that the court poet, Dubthach, and Erc, a
young noble, were forced to stand in his presence. They
were Patrick's first two converts at Tara, Erc later becoming a bishop.

Patrick's teaching and his miracles confounded the
druids. "They can bring darkness," he said of their magic,
"but they cannot bring Light." And he preached Christ to
the court, making converts of the queen and her two
daughters—even some of the druids themselves in
time—and across the years hundreds and thousands of
others.

He worked tirelessly, faced great perils and hardships,
fasted, prayed, built churches, cells, monasteries, con-
vened a synod, ordained priests and bishops, purified and
coded the old law, baptized, confirmed, and celebrated.
He had come to Ireland a Roman and he became an
Irishman. He gave Ireland a new faith and a new soul, and
it gave him the same. Its tongue became his, his spirit
became Ireland's—and each lost its heart to the other. He
died at Down in 460, leaving behind a grief-stricken
people who, as a nation, mourned him for twelve days.

The Breastplate of St. Patrick, is said to have been composed by the saint in the year 433.

I rise up today
Thro' a mighty strength,
Thro' my invocation of the Trinity,
Thro' my belief in its threeness,
Thro' my avowal of its oneness
To the only Creator. . . .

I arise today,
God's strength guiding me,
God's might sustaining me,
God's wisdom directing me,
God's eye looking before me,
God's ear listening to me,
God's word speaking for me,
God's hand protecting me:
The way of God stretching out before me,
The shield of God as my shelter,
The hosts of God guarding me against the snares of the
    demons,
Against the temptings of my evil desire,
Against the evil inclination of my will,
Against everyone who plots against me,
Anear or afar, alone or in a multitude. . . .

Christ with me,
Christ before me,
Christ after me,
Christ within me,
Christ beneath me,
Christ above me,
Christ at my right hand,
Christ at my left hand,
Christ in my breadth,
Christ in my length,
Christ in my height,
Christ in the heart of everyone who thinks of me,
Christ in the mouth of everyone who speaks to me,
Christ in every eye that sees me,
Christ in every ear that hears me. . . .

March 19
Saint Joseph

Although St. Joseph drops out of sight in the Scriptures after the infancy narratives except for an occasional reference to Jesus as "the carpenter's son," we can guess what he was like as an "upright man" from our acquaintance of other such men. Fathers, husbands, brothers, uncles, neighbors, quiet modest men like Joseph whose lives go almost unheeded, reveal, one feels, a resemblance to him—but the best portrait of all is to be found in Jesus, who was formed by him.

Small boys who live and play beside their fathers imitate what they say and do, and it was from hearing the speech of Joseph as well as of Mary that Jesus learned to speak. He heard Joseph lead their prayer morning and evening and tell stories from the Bible. He went to synagogue with him, celebrated feasts with him. He not only learned his craft from Joseph but his attitudes toward work and workers, wages, and people; his love for the poor, for justice, and for freedom. As parents always do for their children, Joseph modeled God for Jesus—his compassion, mercy, justice, tenderness, love—and was a key to Jesus' awareness of himself as Son of God, and of God as Father. It was to Joseph that Jesus first used the Aramaic word for father, *abba*—our equivalent is *daddy*—which, when he used it later for God, revealed an intimacy, tenderness, and playfulness that had never before been expressed. This is a startling revelation in a tradition in which the name of God was never spoken because it was too solemn, too sacred.

The first fragment of Joseph's story is told by Matthew and Luke in the infancy narratives, each quite different and independent of the other. We can presume that he was a young man, not the old gentleman depicted in the largely apochryphal *Protevangelium of James.* Both evangelists identify him as a descendent of David and both agree that he was from Bethlehem, although in Luke's story he has moved to Nazareth and returns only for the census and the birth of Jesus.

Joseph's dilemma when he discovered Mary to be pregnant is not mentioned in Luke but in Matthew it poses an enormous difficulty, the purpose of which was apparently to make clear to the reader that the child was begotten by the Spirit and not through sexual union. One opinion holds that Joseph, as an upright man who honored and kept the law, had no choice but to divorce Mary as the law required, although quietly since he was merciful. Another prefers the theory that, receiving from Mary an explanation of her pregnancy, Joseph felt himself unworthy to be the spouse of one who was so clearly God's sacred vessel. In either case, her pregnancy would have become known and a cause for scandal. But Matthew has everything explained in a dream to Joseph, who then takes Mary to himself as wife. The story of the journey to Bethlehem, the birth of Jesus, the visit of the Magi, the slaughter of innocents, the escape into Egypt and return, serve to confirm Joseph as a gallant husband and protector of Mary and her child. By the time we reach the story of the wedding at Cana, Jesus is called "the son of Mary" which seems to indicate that Joseph has died.

Joseph was called a cutter, a worker in wood, a joiner, since there was no Hebrew word for carpenter, and his work was indispensable to the life of the village. As with all carpenters, he could be recognized by the curled wood shaving he wore behind one ear, although this was always removed on the Sabbath. It was the carpenter's task to fell, cut, and fetch his own wood from the forest, so Joseph would have owned a sturdy donkey to help transport it back to Nazareth. Ilex, oak, pine, cedar, and especially sycamore—which when properly cured, could replace iron as a ploughshare—were the woods he worked with. Olive and vine, when unfruitful, were cut for firewood, and many times Jesus would have heard Joseph assess the uselessness of a tree and "lay the axe to the root" in order to provide for their household (Mt. 3:10; Lk. 13:6–9).

In his workshop facing the street, he prepared beams for houses; jams and lintels for doors; yokes, plows, wheels, frames for straw pallets; chests for clothing; bushel measures; kneading troughs—whatever the villagers needed made out of wood. His tools were the axe, hatchet, saw, knives, adze, plane, square, clamp, hammer, nails, and bow-drill, an import from Egypt. The sounds of these tools at work, the fragrant smell of wood shavings, were part of Jesus' childhood.

"Why look at the speck in your brother's eye when you miss the beam in your own?" (Lk. 6:42) has always seemed such an absurd image until one realizes that a carpenter carrying a beam on his shoulder through the narrow streets of the market was something to watch out for. Did Jesus one day hear Joseph remonstrate a howling injured citizen who was so busy chiding a fellow townsman that he walked right into Joseph's beam?

So many of the everyday things Jesus used to give light to his teaching must have been learned about first in the company of Joseph. Walking beside their donkey as they went to the forest, they would have seen men using the very plows Joseph had made for them, and Joseph would explain that once started, the plowman must never look back or the plow scratching a furrow through the hard rocky soil with so much difficulty might wander and make a crooked line, or even break on a protruding rock. "Whoever puts his hand to the plow but keeps looking back is unfit for the reign of God" (Lk. 9:62).

Did they pass by again as the men swung down the rows casting seed, some of it falling in the plowed earth, some on the hard places, some in the thorns by the road, some on the rock? He would ask about the seed and Joseph would tell him that day and night, as the men rose and slept, the seed would be secretly growing (Mk. 4:26–29). Later seeing weeds among the wheat, would he not also ask about them and remember, long after, Joseph's answer? "Let them both grow together until the harvest; and at harvest time . . . gather up the weeds and bind them in bundles to burn, but the wheat gather into my barn" (Mt. 13:30).

The season went round and one day as they passed the farmer's threshing floor, he would be winnowing. Any child would question to see the farmer toss the threshed wheat into the air with his broad wooden shovel. And Joseph would point out how the wind blew away the chaff—stems, seed husks—and how the heavy grain fell to the ground—"to be gathered into his barn." In Matthew 13:24–30 there is a story he told with that memory in mind.

It was Joseph who explained to him the wisdom of building a house upon rock instead of sand, and Jesus' first acquaintance with fishermen and their nets and with shepherds and their flocks would have been made as he accompanied Joseph through the countryside and down to the lake. He would have taught him about the pruning and manuring of vines, explaining that the townsfolk who lined up at day's end at the vineyard were waiting for their wages. The celebration of the Feast of Tabernacles always came at the time of the new vintage and the preparation of new wineskins, the old being dry and brittle, worn thin from rubbing against the walls of the houses. Did Jesus ask one day, "What happened?" when suddenly some improvident neighbor, too lazy to prepare new skins, found his new wine spilt and wasted on the ground? "No one pours new wine into old wineskins . . ." (Lk. 5:17–39).

Perhaps he remembered Joseph most poignantly that day when he spoke to the crowds about prayer and the loving goodness of God. "But if one of you asks his father for a loaf, will he hand him a stone? or for a fish, will he for a fish hand him a serpent? or if he asks for an egg, will he hand him a scorpion? . . . If you . . . know how to give good gifts to your children, how much more will your heavenly Father give the Good Spirit to those who ask him!" (Lk. 11:9–13).

Matthew follows that passage with: "Therefore all things whatever you would that men should do to you, even so do you also to them; for this is the Law and the Prophets" (Mt. 7:12). And there is Joseph, the "upright man," which means one who lovingly and faithfully clings to the Law and the Prophets, the man who left his mark on the Son of God.

April 16

Saint Benedict Joseph Labre
1748–1783

In the northwest corner of France near the mountains of Flanders lies the village of Amette. There Benedict Joseph Labre was born on March 25, 1748, the eldest of fifteen children of a prosperous farmer, Jean Batiste Labre, and of his wife, Anne Barbe. Loving and pious from the start, Benedict went to the local school and at fourteen, during a spell of hard times, went to live and study with an uncle who was a priest. In the library there, he discovered the sermons of a sixteenth-century preacher, Père Le Jeune, whose unspeakable mortifications, scrupulosity, and preoccupation with hell left an impression on the lad which would last almost to the end of his life.

"Penance alone!" cried this harsh teacher—and it became the grim model for a way of life for Benedict in which lightheartedness and joy were almost total strangers. Not that Benedict was dour, or did not bring God's love to others by his gentleness of soul, but he denied it to himself.

One day, hearing a servant berating some beggars, he recalled a passage from Père Le Jeune: "The chosen soul, when he finds a poor man in the street, filthy, lacerated, wan, stinking and covered with vermin, brings him into his house, sets him near his fire, washes him and puts him to rights; a worldly soul would find this astounding. Whence is the difference? The chosen soul knows the hidden meaning of poverty. . . ." And Benedict suddenly saw the suffering Christ. He emptied his purse, gave the beggars his bread and the food prepared for his next meal—and then heard himself berated by his uncle's irate housekeeper.

One evening, a guest at dinner spoke of the Trappists, and Benedict decided that he must join this strictest (therefore safest?) of the religious orders. But his parents did not agree, and they sent him to live with still another priest uncle, who wisely suggested that the family might find the Carthusians more acceptable. They did, and at nineteen Benedict Joseph Labre was allowed to start on his quest of vocation.

But the Carthusians at Longueness turned him down, as did those at Montreuil. He returned home to complete his studies, went back to Montreuil and was accepted, but they let him go when, in time, a terrible depression possessed him. Convinced now that La Trappe was his destiny, he started off for the Trappists only to be turned down. He returned home in the depths of winter, ragged, exhausted, desolate. Home for a year, working, reading, praying, longing to expiate the evil in the world, he asked his bishop's permission to try again. "Go to the Carthusians!" he was told. He did and was again turned away. In October, his family received a letter saying he was once more setting out for the Trappists, asking their forgiveness and bidding them read and heed Père Le Jeune—"If you do not, you have no hope of salvation; meditate on the horrors of hell; try hard to be among the few who are chosen." What a strange, merciless vision of God!

Turned away again, he was at last accepted by the Trappists at Septfonts where his name was changed to Friar Urban. At first his heart was filled with joy, but soon the darkness closed in again. His prayer froze, he refrained from receiving communion, he revealed his agony of soul—and they sent him away. Seven times he had been turned away.

Now, in the company of beggars, thieves, exiles, the despised of society, he tramped the roads to the shrines, praying to know his vocation. With Christ, he accepted blows, insults, deprivations, and practiced austerities more demanding than any monk's—and he discovered his vocation was to be a beggar, a tramp. He wanted nothing but the condition of the abject poor. His life became the random journey of a mangy dog, poking through refuse for the next crust, orange peel, wilted cabbage leaf—always in search of God.

What did he look like? He was young, his beard was short and fair, even reddish, his hair came to his shoulders, his face was hollow-cheeked and white, his eyes innocent and peaceful. He wore rags, a disreputable three-cornered hat, a rosary about his neck, and buckled shoes that were falling apart. His pilgrim's pack was stuffed with passports, holy cards, medals, pinches of soil from shrines, pamphlets on death, the *Imitation of Christ,* and a volume of *Luis de Granada.* He stank and was infested with vermin, which he at first tried to be rid of, but in the end he submitted to being their host, as though even the most loathsome of God's creatures had a right to their sustenance. Eventually he carried a bell to warn people away.

Rarely would he consent to bathe (although once, in spite of not knowing how to swim, he jumped in a river and rescued a child). He spoke gracefully and was well-mannered at table. Mothers brought their children to him for blessing until, when he realized that this bordered on veneration, he would disappear. Priests hearing his confession discovered a soul residing on the heights of mysticism.

Once in Fabriano, a woman asked him to see a young invalid who was hoping for a cure. Instead, he opened up to her the mystery of vicarious suffering. "To love God," he said, "You need three hearts in one: a heart of fire for Him; a heart of flesh for your neighbor, and a heart of bronze for yourself." Little by little, the Lord was transforming his own fearful vision. The time would come when someone would ask, "What would you do if an angel came and told you that you were condemned?" "I would have confidence," was his answer.

During the winter of 1773, he lived in an attic in Moulins, leaving each morning at dawn to spend the day in prayer in the collegiate church. There the pastor became suspicious of this solitary loitering figure and visited his landlord to warn him, only to learn that the fellow stayed up whole nights in prayer as well and ate only a few peas and bits of toast soaked in water. That year on Maundy Thursday Benedict collected twelve beggars as dirty as himself and brought them to his attic to share his meager store of crusts and peas. Snickering, they held out their bowls, Benedict lifted up his offerings as though in consecration, and he became transfigured. He had enough food to fill their bowls to the brim. Pressed to explain, he answered vaguely, "I have a patron. . . ." When the pastor heard, he concluded that the "patron" could only be accounted for by a recent theft, and he warned his landlord that there would be a police investigation. Benedict, hearing of this, disappeared.

Once he came upon a man half dead from a beating by robbers. Taking what rags he had in his possession, he found a stream and was washing the man's wounds when two passing horsemen took him to be one of the robbers and dragged him off to jail. Only when the man recovered was Benedict identified as his savior. Once, outside the prison in Bari, he sang the Litany of Our Lady and begged for coins. Then he gave what he had collected to the prisoners who were thrusting their hands through the barred windows over their heads.

In seven years, he traveled to all the chief shrines of Europe, and after six journeys to Rome, he decided to stay there. He became known as the holy beggar who lived in the Colosseum, stood last in line for food at the convents, and gave his place to anyone who came later than he. He stood on the porches of churches and saw into the hearts of the worshipers, speaking to them of their secret injustice, impurity, envy, jealousy. "But God will not abandon you," he told them. One morning before dawn he prayed at the Church of the Madonna de Monti and a young girl, seeing the figure haloed in light before the altar, thought the sun was shining on him. When she went out of the church she found it was still dark night. Another time he was seen suspended above the floor before the high altar at San Ignacio. The sacristan, sweeping nearby, calmly replied to an astonished visitor, "The saint is in ecstasy," and went on sweeping.

In time he sacrificed his privacy and moved into a hostel with twelve other beggars, so influencing them that in time they arose in the night to say the Divine Office. But other beggars of Rome hated him and lost no occasion to curse him, to throw stones at him and beat him. He was so secretive about receiving Communion that some priests called him a Jansenist, until it became known that he received the sacrament at the earliest Masses in the most remote churches, and was often haloed by light.

In the spring, he went to Loreto and stayed with the only family from whom he would accept decent clothing or enjoy a taste of good food. Back in Rome, he became as emaciated as ever, the familiar bundle of rags huddled behind a pillar gazing at the tabernacle. Only now he was filled with joy, his face luminous, his smile ecstatic. The last year of his life he confessed to a priest that he was free at last of all temptation, even the temptation to sorrow.

Wednesday of Holy Week in 1783, on his way back from services, he could no longer even stagger, and a butcher took him in and put him to bed. "You are tired, Benedict. You need to sleep." And he spoke his last words. "Yes, I am tired. I want to go to sleep." Within hours he was dead, and by morning the people of Rome had risen up "like an earthquake" to honor him.

Even in death, he was in tatters. The clean white garment with which they clothed his body was plucked and torn by souvenir seekers, even bits of his hair and beard were stolen. And there occurred that phenomenon so common to the deaths of the saints—little children filled the street crying, "The saint is dead! The saint is dead!" It was April 16, and Benedict was thirty-five years old, a strange and disturbing saint, but a gentle and loving one—a special friend to all the wanderers of our times.

April 21

Saint Anselm
1033–1109

St. Anslem, Archbishop of Canterbury, was an Italian from Piedmont, born into a noble family in Aostia in 1033, the son of a deeply religious mother and a father somewhat less so. As a child, he had a dream of climbing a very high mountain and entering the halls of the court of God, where he was fed a wondrous bread by the king himself. It was a dream about which he often spoke throughout his life, which was not unlike an arduous mountain climb.

Sent to a monastery school before he was five, the regimen of studies, long hours, and harsh discipline drove him perilously close to a breakdown. His tutor, in his desire to make a prodigy of this very small, very bright boy, finally had to send him home in a state little short of derangement.

Long after, Anselm responded to an abbot who complained of failure with his students: "If you planted a tree in your garden, and bound it on all sides so that it could not spread its branches, what kind of tree would it prove to be when in after years you gave it room to spread? . . . But that is how you treat your boys . . . cramping them with fears and blows, debarring them also from the enjoyment of any freedom." Seven hundred years later another Piedmontese, John Bosco, would hold the same views and they would seem as bizarre and innovative to his contemporaries.

At fifteen, Anselm wanted to enter a monastery but his father, fancying a bishop son rather than a monk, demurred. At the death of his mother he finally left home, studied briefly in Burgundy and then went on to Bec, attracted by the fame of the great Italian abbot Lanfranc. He became a Benedictine monk at twenty-seven and when Lanfranc moved on to Caen, Anselm became the prior of Bec. During his stay there, he wrote the first of the many works which would earn him the titles of the Father of Scholasticism and Doctor of the Church, and would rank him as an equal of Augustine and Thomas Aquinas.

In 1078, when Anselm became abbot of Bec, he was often required to visit England where Lanfranc was now Archbishop of Canterbury. At the latter's death in 1089, the king—son of William the Conqueror and called William Rufus because of his red hair—refused to fill the see in order to keep the revenues for himself. When illness put the fear of death in him, he promised to observe the law and he nominated Anselm archbishop. Anselm pleaded ill health and unfitness but the bishops forced the pastoral staff into his hand and bore him away to the church themselves singing the *Te Deum* as they went.

Rufus recovered from both his illness and his change of heart, and doubled the levy on Canterbury in an effort to raise money for war. Anselm, when told that the traditional payment of five hundred pounds was not enough, gave the money to the poor. In addition, he admonished the king to fill the vacant and impoverished abbeys, to convene a synod to stop abuses among the clergy, and the enraged king tried unsuccessfully to depose him. William was even angrier when the pallium, insignia of the archbishopric, arrived from Rome and Anselm refused to permit the king to invest him in the office. (The struggle between the church and the kings over investiture was an ongoing battle for years.) Instead, Anselm walked down the aisle of the church robed but barefoot, took the pallium from the altar and put it on himself.

As a consequence of all this, Anselm and the king were now bitter enemies, and when the archbishop started out for Rome to enlist the protection of the Holy See, he was stopped at the seacoast by order of the king and searched to see if he were stealing treasure of the realm. All across Europe he was threatened by both nobles and brigands, each supposing him to be a rich ecclesiastic who could be easily robbed. He finally traveled not only poorly but in disguise.

Anselm returned to England at the death of Rufus to be wildly welcomed by the people and by Rufus's brother Henry, the new king, whose bride was Matilda, the daughter of St. Margaret of Scotland. Henry proved no better than Rufus and he and Anselm came to an impasse over the same old issues. Anselm returned to Rome and Henry exiled him. Only the threat of excommunication effected a reconciliation—in which, one suspects, Matilda had a hand. In time, however, Henry came to trust Anselm implicitly.

St. Anselm was one of the first to oppose slavery. In 1102 he fostered the passing of a resolution in the national council of Westminster prohibiting the practice of "selling men like cattle." He was known for his sermons, which were pointed up with homely illustrations that even the simplest people could understand. He lived to the age of seventy-five, a man of great charm, sympathy, and sincerity. He was deeply loved and grieved by people of all classes and nationalities. He died on April 21, 1109.

April 29

Saint Catherine of Siena
1347–1380

Catherine of Siena was a twin, the twenty-fourth of twenty-five children. She was born in Siena in 1347 on the Feast of the Annunciation. Her father, Giacomo Benincasa, was a prominent dyer and a kind man; her mother, Lapa, a practical woman but inclined to be a shrew. Though not a beauty, she was a merry little girl with unusual golden brown hair, and everyone called her Euphrosyne, probably after one of the desert saints whose stories she loved to hear.

At the age of six, Catherine saw a vision of Christ over the Dominican church in Siena and lost her heart forever. From that moment she decided not to marry, but she did not tell her family and, when in her teens she refused to set her cap for a husband, her mother called in one of the Dominican fathers, her adopted brother Thomas della Fonte, to persuade her. Failing, he remarked as he left, "If you really don't want to marry, why not cut off your hair? No one will want to marry you." So she did.

In a fury, her mother dismissed the servants, set Catherine to do all the work of the household so she would have no time to pray, and took away her room so she would have no place to pray. But the Lord came to Catherine and told her that if she would simply "turn inward to the cell of your own soul," there would be both the time and the place to find him always. He taught her to respond to her family's harassment by imagining that she was serving him, his mother, his brethren, and she would be able to serve them sweetly.

Puzzled, her father finally realized that her strange resolve flowed from a genuine, if bewildering, vocation and he left her free to live as she wished. She was permitted to withdraw to her own cell-like room in solitude where she could pray, fast, and keep silence. Often enraptured in prayer, she was also tormented by temptations, and to her complaints that he had abandoned her, Jesus answered, "I am always with you in your heart, strengthening you." Eventually she experienced what is called "mystical espousal," a rapturous experience in which Christ in the presence of the Virgin Mary placed a ring on her finger.

After three years of seclusion, Jesus bade Catherine go out and serve him in the world, but she protested that she was too weak, the world too evil. "The only way you can serve me, Catherine, is in your service of your neighbor," was the reply, and after that there was no holding back.

She took food and clothing to the poor—always at night to save them humiliation—and in the hospitals she nursed the most abandoned and repulsive of patients.

There was a woman named Tecca whose condition was so repelling that no one would go near her. Catherine heard this and went to care for her with tender love, for which Tecca was grateful at first. But soon she took a dislike to this "saint" and spread rumors assailing not only her motives but her virginity until Catherine was the subject of vicious gossip throughout the city of Siena. Catherine wept, and one night Christ appeared holding a crown of gold and a crown of thorns. "Choose the one you want for this life, Catherine," he said, "and I will save the other for eternity." She remembered, she said, that even as he was dying for love of his enemies, they were reviling him, and she said, "I want to be like you." She took the crown of thorns, asking that the wounds remain invisible, as they were until her death. Then he promised that her faithful service of Tecca would be precisely the prayer that would win the woman's repentance. One morning as Catherine entered her room, Tecca seemed to see instead of Catherine the face of Christ, and she wept and was reconciled.

One day, as Catherine left the Dominican church in Siena, a beggar cried out for alms but she had nothing to give him. If he would go home with her, she said, she could give him clothes and food and money. He replied that he had no time to go with her; he wanted something then and there. She had only a little metal cross at the end of a string knotted for counting prayers, and he took that and went off, bowing and blessing her. That night Christ came to her and he was the beggar. Holding up the cross now studded with jewels, he asked, "Catherine, do you recognize this?" "Ah yes, Lord," she said, "but it did not look like that when I gave it to you." "No," he replied, "your love has done this to it. And I will give it back to you on judgment day in front of angels and men to show how you have loved me."

She was indefatigable in her ministering. She cared for the plague-ridden (carrying a bottle of scent to overcome the stench), buried the dead, visited prisons, and even received into her hands the head of an executed knight. She was so gifted at healing feuds and touching consciences that three Dominican priests were appointed to hear the confessions of those she brought to penitence.

Convinced that only some common and noble cause could reunite the warring factions in the church and purify its corruption, she was a passionate supporter of a crusade to retake Jerusalem from the Saracens. This undertaking was interrupted, however, when five city states formed a league against the Holy See and Catherine was called upon to go to the papal court in Avignon as peacemaker. Once there, she was made to play the fool as the Florentines disclaimed her and the Pope ignored her. Nevertheless, the journey was not fruitless; for the seventh time she remonstrated with Gregory XI to return to Rome, and this time she prevailed. After almost 75 years in France, the papacy moved back where it belonged.

Home again, Catherine urged Gregory to rid the church of scandalous prelates and to make peace with Florence, only to have him repudiate her angrily and break off their friendship. It was at this time that she dictated her great spiritual classic, *The Dialogue,* in which is found the substance of her conversations with Christ. As the work of a totally uneducated woman dictated to secretaries—she could not write—this work is a phenomenon of theological wisdom filled with original ideas and imagery. Among the many insights she received from the Lord, the famous image of the continuous presence of God was: "As the fish is in the sea, so thou art in me and I am in thee. . . ." This work as much as anything else accounts for her title as Doctor of the Church.

Gregory died and Urban was elected Pope. The rebellious French cardinals, their hearts still in France, then elected their own pope, and the church was rent in two. Having effected the return of the papacy from Avignon, Catherine was now blamed, and blamed herself, for this new calamity. At the request of Urban, she hurried to Rome with her group of followers to counsel, encourage, and support him in his struggle to end the schism. She dictated hundreds of letters to the world's mighty, seeking their support for Urban, and the tide seemed to change in his favor only to change as quickly again. Supporters disappeared, bloody battles broke out, lifelong friends turned away from Catherine—even, temporarily, her beloved director Raymond of Capua. Worst of all, she began to see Urban change and become indifferent, suspicious, cruel.

Constantly suffering, not only from her own austerities and the stigmata that she had received in prayer but also from the ghastly decadence in the church, Catherine's health broke altogether. She was wracked with pain, demonic torments darkened her spirit, and once she "died" and left her body, seeming to see it as though it were another's, only to return to it after the Lord had spoken to her of the needs of the church. In her last struggle, as she lay dying, she cried out as though to an opponent: "Never vainglory! But true glory in Christ crucified!" It was April 29, 1380. She was thirty-three years old and her ministry, like Christ's, seemed a failure. And, like him, she would emerge in history to dwarf her enemies and her detractors.

It was because Catherine of Siena saw with the vision of the Gospels that she demolished every notion of what a woman ought to do and be in the Middle Ages—not because she was consciously fighting a battle for sexual freedom; to her, in Christ there was no difference. The masculine and the feminine in her nature were so perfectly melded that she remains a model of what it means to be free of stereotypes. She could make and send the pope sugared, gilded oranges as a Christmas confection, with a note encouraging him to discover that beyond the first bitter taste he would find sweetness—much as one finds sweetness in the will of God. And she could remonstrate with the same pope with the daring and force of an archangel. Freedom and equality for everyone is implicit in the teaching of Jesus, and for Catherine this meant that she had to do what she had to do. That she was a woman had little to do with it. The church has still to learn the lesson.

May 3

Saint James the Less and Saint Philip the Apostle
First Century

St. James the Less hardly appears in the Gospels until after the death of Jesus and is certainly less than inspiring when he does. To be honest, he is more like us than like the saints. There are three Jameses in the Gospels, and identifying James the Less is very difficult. The *Jerome Biblical Commentary* has this to say:

"Among Jesus' acquaintances, we seem to have three men named James: (1) James son of Zebedee, 'the Greater' (meaning older or taller) one of the Twelve; (2) James son of Alphaeus, one of the Twelve; (3) James, presumably son of Clophas, 'the Less' (meaning younger or smaller) (Mk. 15:40) a 'brother' of Jesus, later 'bishop' of Jerusalem, traditional author of an epistle, an apostle in the broad sense of the word (Gal. 1:19), but not one of the Twelve."

We meet James the Less first when Jesus' family, hearing that huge crowds were following him and he did not even have time to eat, "came to take charge of him, saying 'He's out of his mind' " (Mk. 3:20–22). When they arrived at the house where Jesus was and were announced to the Lord as his mother and brothers, Jesus answered, "Who is my mother? Who are my brothers? He looked at the people sitting around him and said, "Look! Here are my mother and my brothers! Whoever does what God wants him to do is my brother, my sister, my mother!" (Mk. 3:20–35). James the Less was one of this family group.

He appears again toward the end of Jesus' public life, at the time of the Feast of Tabernacles, when Jesus' brothers said to him, "Leave this place and go to Judea, so that your disciples will see the work you are doing. No one hides what he is doing if he wants to be well-known. Since you are doing these things, let the whole world know about you" (Jn. 7:1–9). A disappointing picture of them all, it ends with a parenthesis: "(Not even his brothers believed in him.)"

Nothing more is heard of James the Less until after the Resurrection, when Paul mentions him briefly in an account of Jesus' appearances before his Ascension: "Then he appeared to James" (1 Cor. 15:7). There is a bit in the apochryphal *Gospel of the Hebrews* which seems to relate to this. A story there tells that after the death of Jesus, James made a vow that he would neither eat nor drink until he saw Jesus again, and that Jesus did appear to him. What Jesus could not do for James in life, his death seemed to do, giving him an understanding of things which at first had seemed like madness. Only after James saw Jesus die did he discover who he was and dedicate his life to him.

James is mentioned only three more times, but he is a

changed man now, a Jewish Christian who has left temerity and indecision behind and is no longer afraid. When Paul went back to Jerusalem three years after his conversion, he did not see any of the apostles except Peter and James, "the Lord's brother" (Gal. 1:19). The others were still suspicious of him, but not Peter and James.

When Peter escaped from prison and arrived at the home of Mary, the mother of John Mark, he told the story of his escape and then directed his listeners to "Tell these tidings to James and the brethren" (Acts 12:12–17). So James is now recognized as a leader in the community.

And when in 49 or 50, a dispute arose over circumcision for Gentiles which required a meeting of apostles and elders in Jerusalem, we hear from James again. After Peter's statement that salvation comes by the grace of Christ and not by externals, James wrote to the Gentile Christians that circumcision was not necessary; but, conservative that he was, he still held them to their dietary laws (Acts 15:1–35).

The rest of his story is tradition. Hegesippus, author of *The Gospel of the Hebrews,* says James was called "the Just," so highly esteemed was he. It was said that from his birth, he had no wine or strong drink, meat, haircuts, anointing with oil, or baths (!); that he wore only linen; and that he prayed in the Temple (the first Christians remained practicing Jews for some time) so often that "the skin of his knees was like a camel's." He was responsible for so many converts that the scribes and Pharisees were alarmed. They persuaded him to stand on the pinnacle of the Temple to speak to the people at Passover and then they pushed him off. When that failed to kill him, they stoned him, and when stoning failed, they prevailed upon a fuller (weaver) who was standing by to bludgeon him to death with his fuller's bat. Josephus, the Jewish historian, holds the date to have been A.D. 62. That he shares a feast with

St. Philip is probably because Pope John III in 570 dedicated a church in their honor.

James the Less is not listed as a special patron for anyone, but together with Philip he might well be the patron of all of us as the meaning of the coming of Jesus becomes clearer and moves us to make our lives visibly, boldly Christian.

Saint Philip is referred to only eight times in all of the Gospels, a startling reminder that the men to whom we owe the most are the least known of all the saints. And Philip the Apostle is especially little known. He appears in the story the day after Andrew and Peter have met Jesus.

"The following day Jesus decided to go into Galilee. He found Philip and said to him, 'Come with me!' " Philip did, and when the day was over he went to find Nathaniel and told him: "We have found the one of whom Moses wrote in the book of the Law, and of whom the Prophets wrote also. He is Jesus, the son of Joseph, from Nazareth." To Nathaniel's flippant query about what good could come out of Nazareth, Philip simply said, "Come and see" (Jn. 1:43–46).

This bit tells much about Philip. He could not explain his conviction, but he knew that if Nathaniel could meet Jesus, he would see for himself. Philip is not stupid, but Jesus is unique, so new and so different that he is impossible to explain.

Philip appears again at the multiplication of the loaves and fishes in John 6:1–15. Jesus had tried to withdraw from the crowds by sailing across the Sea of Galilee, a distance of about four miles. The people were determined to stay with him, however, and seeing where he was bound, they circled around the top of the lake by land and met him on the other side. He was making for the very town that was the home of Philip, Peter, and Andrew,

about two miles up the Jordan from where it flows into the
sea.

Some distance from the shore there was a grassy plain.
Jesus and his disciples had disappeared around a hill behind the plain when the crowd found them. Jesus, knowing they had walked many miles to get there, realized how
hungry they must be. He turned to Philip, who knew the
district and what provisions it might have, and asked,
"Where are we to buy bread for these to eat?" Philip's
answer was not hopeful. "Two hundred denarii of bread is
not enough for them, that each one may receive a little."
Two hundred denarii was the equivalent of six months'
wages for one man reckoned at a denarius a day. Obviously they did not have so much money.

To be unimaginative is perhaps difficult, but it is not a
fault. Creative people have a constant stream of new ideas
and can easily improvise. Others cannot, and Philip was
one of the latter. Andrew, for example, knew intuitively
that there must be an answer somewhere. He went scout-
ing around and found the boy with the barley loaves and
the fishes. Even these were not enough, but Andrew was
expectant. It is comforting to know that the Lord chose
such ordinary people for his intimates.

On another occasion later on, when Jesus was in
Jerusalem for the Passover, some inquiring Greek visitors
wanted to meet him (Jn. 12:20–22). Perhaps they had
been present at the Temple the day he castigated the
moneychangers, or perhaps they had simply heard about
him and were intrigued. They went to Philip—logically,
since he had a Greek name—but Philip, uncertain, referred them to Andrew. Philip was a careful man; his only
rash moment was that first unforgettable instant when
Jesus called to him and he threw caution to the winds and
went. Looking back, one sees it as an heroic act of faith.
Philip was a man of faith, not vision.

At the Last Supper, after Jesus' announcement that he

was leaving to prepare a place for them, Thomas asked about "the way" to where he was going. Jesus replied that *he* was the way. "If you have known me, you would also have known my Father. And henceforth, you do know him, and you have seen him" (Jn. 14:1–14). And Philip leaned forward eagerly and asked, "Lord, show us the Father," almost as if Jesus had brought a few slides with him and was now going to show them a picture of God.

It is such a revealing request. His expectation that the Father had a face and a form and could be seen as Jesus could be seen, is like ours. Twenty centuries after, it is hard for people to erase the image of God as the old man with the long white beard that appeared on the pages of the religion texts until such a short time ago. When Jesus said, "Philip, who sees me sees the Father," one understands his bewilderment. Philip had to put together bit by bit, piece by piece, a new idea of God. After Pentecost it would become clearer to him that the Christ is man for our sakes, because we can only really know God if he is like us. Jesus *is* what the Father is like—his love, his concern, his truth, his goodness, and his insistence that in dying we do not die.

There is not much more known of Philip except what we know of the apostles as a group. He is named with the others as they await Pentecost in the Upper Room and that is the last we see of him. It is even disputed whether he was martyred or died a natural death. That he had three daughters we learn from the bishop of Ephesus in the second century, who reports that two had lived as virgins all their lives in Hierapolis, and the third in Ephesus.

St. Philip is not listed as the patron of anyone in particular except those who bear his name, but he seems rather to be a patron of us all as we struggle to understand ever more clearly the mystery of God revealed in Jesus. It certainly seems appropriate that his feast day be celebrated with sardine sandwiches.

May 12

Saint Nereus
and Saint Achilleus
First Century

Here are two saints about whom so little is known that only the inscription on their tombstones survive. Their legendary "acts" claim them to have been attendants in the household of a noble Christian lady, Flavia Domitilla, who was a distant niece by marriage to the emperor, Domition Together with others, they suffered during his persecution of the Christians. According to St. Jerome, she and her household were banished to the island of Ponza (a fate Jerome seemed to regard as martyrdom enough). In time, Nereus and Achilleus were supposedly beheaded during the persecution of the emperor Trajan, while Domitilla was burned at the stake because she refused to sacrifice to idols. All three were buried in a family vault in the catacomb that has become known as the cemetery of Domitilla. It is from the tombstone found there that the only bit of true biography for Nereus and Achilleus is found, written in excellent verse by Pope St. Damasus who diligently searched the records for accurate accounts of the martyrs.

This epitaph reads: "The martyrs Nereus and Achilleus had enrolled themselves in the army and exercised the cruel office of carrying out the orders of the tyrant, being ever ready through the constraint of fear to obey his will. O miracle of faith! Suddenly they cease from their fury, they become converted, they fly from the camp of their wicked leader; they throw away their shields, their armour, and their bloodstained javelins. Confessing the faith of Christ, they rejoice to bear testimony to its triumph. Learn now from the words of Damasus what great things the glory of Christ can accomplish."

To embrace Christianity meant one could no longer go to war. Christians were forbidden to bear arms, so the only way out for Nereus and Achilleus was escape, thus compounding their crimes—which were to love Christ and witness for peace.

May 26
Saint Philip Neri
1515–1595

P hilip Neri, born in Florence on July 21, 1515, was the son of Leonardo Neri, an impoverished notary, and his wife Lucrezia, who died when her son was only five. But her faith and character left their stamp on this merry little boy who, raised by a stepgrandmother, was such a delightful child that everyone called him *Pippo Buono*— good little Pippo.

At eighteen, he left Florence and went to San Germano (Cassino today) to live with an uncle who had a small business he wanted to leave to him. But the Benedictines at Monte Cassino seem to have had their effect, and several months later he thanked his uncle and left for Rome. He was not quite sure what he was to do there but it had something to do with serving God.

In Rome, he lived in the attic room of a Florentine family named Caccia, in return for which he tutored their two little boys. He took his board in flour and olives, had his bread baked at the public oven, watered his wine, even drank plain water—an unheard of austerity in an Italian city. In his room he had a bed, some books, and a line on

which he hung his clothes; always fastidiously clean, he
wore only plain garments of linen and wool, never silk.

He enrolled at the university to study philosophy and
theology but, although he was a brilliant student, he knew
after three years that his vocation was not there. He sold
his books, gave away the money to poor students, and
turned his attention to prayer, visiting the more forgotten
churches of Rome where it was quiet, spending days at a
time in the catacombs of San Sebastian. He was twenty-
three.

What happened in the catacombs is not entirely clear,
but much later an aged Oratorian revealed something
Philip had confided about his experiences there. One day
while praying, he seemed to see a ball of fire roll swiftly
down from heaven straight into his mouth and sink into his
heart. From that moment a fire burned in his breast caus-
ing such heat to emanate, although without pain, that he
had to wear the lightest clothing even in winter. Often
when he was absorbed in prayer, his whole body—indeed
the furniture and the very room itself—would shake. A
large swelling appeared in the region of his heart, and after
his death an autopsy revealed the fracture of two ribs in
the chest cavity and the distortion of the cartilage over the
heart. The doctors consulted by Benedict XIV concluded
that the enlargement was caused by an aneurism, which
itself could have been caused by his mystical experience.
His penitents testified that often, when he would hold
their heads to his breast, a great peace would penetrate
them and temptation would disappear.

A layman and unmarried, he felt increasingly called to a
ministry to the young men of Rome. It was a time of lush
humanism when many young people who were at least
nominally Christian were caught up in an unrestrained celebration of the senses, yet at the same time were drawn by
a yearning for mysticism, that strange combination of car-

nal passion and idealism which seems to characterize not just the late Renaissance but even our own times. Philip took to wandering the streets, playing quoits, stopping by banks where young clerks gathered. He was witty and pleasant and had a gift for touching a sensitive spot with a single remark. Often he would approach a group of young men and say, "Well, my friends, when are we going to begin to do good?"

He visited the poor and abandoned in the hospitals, made their beds, cleaned them of filth, brought gifts of fruit and cakes—probably from his friends in the shops—and inevitably he gathered a following. With his confessor, he formed a confraternity to serve the poor who journeyed to Rome during the jubilee year, supporting a hospice where in time even popes went to serve food and to wash feet. Long after, when John Henry Newman was about to enter the Oratory in 1847, he would also do so, finding it a bit romantic but nevertheless remarking that the task was a real one—"the feet needed washing." And finally, when Philip was thirty-five, having far more education than was required at the time, he succumbed to the persistent urgings that he be ordained. He then moved to the priests' residence at San Girolamo della Carità, where he would live for thirty years.

San Girolamo's maintained a team of resident priest chaplains and rented rooms to still other clergy who paid their own expenses; Philip was one of these. His few possessions consisted of some books and the accustomed attire—a gown with long sleeves almost to the ground (rough cloth without linen cuffs), a biretta, and a big hat. His large "white" shoes, so-called because they were the cheaper undyed raw leather, became an object of ridicule which he bore good-humoredly, mindful that pride could not survive if one could laugh at one's self.

Tension was already high at San Girolamo because one

of the priests had introduced the unheard of practice of giving daily Communion to the faithful (and to women, no less)! With Philip's appearance and his frequent, sometimes daily, penitents, it became worse, and the two were soon the butt of much ill will and persecution. Two sacristans in particular tormented Philip mercilessly, putting out shabby vestments, dirty Mass vessels (for years he had a fixation about drinking out of dirty cups), locking the sacristy, and deliberately misplacing the key to the tabernacle. When he complained one day in prayer to the Lord, "When will you send me patience?" the reply was, "Philip, you will acquire patience precisely by putting up with these two." And he did, in the end winning them as loyal followers.

Soon men were coming to him in flocks, from early morning to late night—tailors, bankers, herbalists, perfumers, goldsmiths, hosiers, carpenters, barbers, shoemakers, booksellers, cowkeepers, the scions of noble families, and thieves, brigands and usurers. Soon their unstructured and informal gatherings became spiritual conferences, with readings, discussions, talks, visits to churches, even pilgrimages with picnics. When they outgrew his little room, Philip took over the loft above the church, creating an oratory that gave its name not only to the place and the group but to the music he asked his musician friends to compose for these evenings. Palestrina wrote oratories for Philip Neri's evenings with his friends.

But Philip Neri is probably best known for his use of teasing and ridicule to teach his penitents humility and simplicity. Always sensitive to the limitations of each individual, Philip nevertheless preferred the barbed quip, the comical task, the ludicrous posture to other more sober mortifications. One young man asked Philip's permission to wear a hair shirt, to which Philip agreed, specifying "on the outside." A foppish, spoiled young noble was told to carry his fat little spaniel through the streets, and another to balance a rooster on his elegant hat. So easily did Philip slip into ecstasy that he had to read a chapter or two of his favorite joke book in order to keep his feet on the ground before Mass.

He directed women at a time when they were considered far too dangerous for virtuous priests to chance—and several were. He was called to the bedside of a woman who he was told wanted to confess, only to find one of the famous courtesans of Rome stretched out on her couch invitingly. He turned and fled. Another time he was accosted by two young men who tried their seductions on him, but he overwhelmed them with his own kind of love and they became his disciples.

In time, he singled out five followers (among them a young man who would one day become the eminent historian Baronius), drew up a simple rule of life, and they became the Congregation of the Oratory. They shared a common table, had spiritual exercises under his direction but no vows, nor did they give up their property, if any. Because by this time all of Rome knew of him—his cures, his conversions, his ability to read hearts and foresee events—it is no surprise that jealousy in high Vatican circles should breed suspicion. But equally high friends came to his rescue, among them the young Cardinal of Milan, Charles Borromeo. Eventually all was well again.

He was the friend of cardinals, popes, saints—Ignatius of Loyola, Camillus de Lellis, Felix of Cantalice, Francis de Sales—and when he was finally given a ruined church for his own, they, together with the poor and the lowly, contributed so he could build a new one. He was called "the Apostle of Rome," so great was the role he played in converting the corrupt and powerful in the church and out of it—this man who could not bear to see carcasses hanging in butcher shops, and who always let his pet birds be free, although they never flew away.

He died at eighty. Two weeks earlier he had received

viaticum and had said, "I have never done anything good, not a thing." He rallied for a time and on his favorite feast, Corpus Christi, sitting on his bed, he closed his eyes, sighed, and was gone. It was May 25, 1595.

May 30

Saint Joan of Arc
1412–1431

The story of Joan of Arc begins with the bastard Dauphin Charles VII, the weak-eyed, knobby-kneed, spindle-legged heir to the throne of France, beleaguered in the small city of Bourges while the English invaders crowned their own infant king in Paris. The powerful dukes of Burgundy, long contenders in a civil war with the dukes of Orléans, had thrown in their lot with the English, so that France was not only torn by a foreign enemy but by Frenchmen fighting Frenchmen as well—as always, it was the people who suffered. Plagued for eighty of the Hundred Years' War by famine, looting, raping, burning, their misery could not have been worse.

Then out of the valley of the Meuse rose the memory of a prophecy, said to have been spoken first by Merlin, that a virgin would come from the forests of Lorraine to lead the king to victory and restore France to her people. Not only

Joan but her church examiners at Poitier, where she was interrogated before the march to Orléans, were convinced that her call was its fulfillment.

She was born in Domrémy in 1412 to the farm family of Jacques and Isabelle Darc—a name which a French poet would later change to *d'Arc*. Joan was a cheerful girl, probably rather plain, who preferred to work in the house—no one in all Domrémy was her equal at embroidery—but because she was sturdy and strong she was more often tending sheep, cows, pigs, or riding bareback in the fields helping her father and brothers. When it came time for her to go off to war, her noble companions envied the way she rode. She could not read or write but she knew her prayers, loved God, and from her mother learned by heart the stories of the saints.

It was in the spring of her thirteenth year that the adventure began. She was in her father's garden when suddenly bells rang, a bright light descended, and she knelt and heard a voice tell her not to be afraid. A few days later it spoke again, and the third time she recognized St. Michael the Archangel. He told her to be good, to go to church, and that soon St. Catherine and St. Margaret, virgin martyrs whose stories she knew well, would come to guide her. Each time she was bathed in the light such peace and loveliness engulfed her that she wept when the voices left her.

Catherine of Alexandria and Margaret of Antioch came, crowned and in dazzling garments, and over the next five years their voices spoke to her as many as three times a week. Like them she vowed to remain a maid always, belonging to God and serving him. From a boisterous girl who loved to beat the village boys at races, she became quiet and thoughtful, spending her free time in prayer. Guided by her confessor as well as her heavenly visitors, little by little she was drawn into the mystical life. But it was a mysticism marked by the most practical, healthy behavior, and by extreme tenderness toward the suffering and the unfortunate.

In time she was told of three tasks entrusted to her: to save the city of Orléans from the English, to see the Dauphin crowned king at Rheims, and to drive the English from France. Then one day her voices commanded her to begin. Persuading the commandant at Vaucouleurs to give her an escort, she started the dangerous journey south through enemy territory to the Dauphin at Chinon, dressed in male clothing and with her hair cropped. She wore men's clothes, she said, so her soldier companions would feel no desire for her, and so she could guard her virginity in thought and deed. She rode beside them and slept beside them, but the duke of Alençon, who remarked that she had shapely breasts, could say that he was never tempted by her. So could her chief of staff, and Dunois, brother to the duke of Orléans, who testified that "no woman could be more chaste than *La Pucelle.*" This was the name by which all France came to know her—the maid, the virgin.

At Chinon she went to the Dauphin with the simplicity of a shepherd girl. "I have been sent from God to bring help to the kingdom and yourself," she told him. Timorous and unconvinced, after much delay Charles decided to have church officials at Poitier examine the orthodoxy of her beliefs. At the same time his thoroughly decadent, enormously obese mother insisted that a group of court ladies confirm Joan's sex and virginity. Whether she was male, female, or hermaphrodite was the question. Through it all, Joan kept her head and answered with such tart intelligence that she may even then have sown the seeds of their final resentment.

Did Joan of Arc really command the armies of France or was she more important for the inspiration she brought? It is still debated. Frequently she led military operations which ought not to have succeeded but did, and there is no doubt that her presence was the key to raising the siege of Orléans. The next day, on the feast of St. Michael, she gave thanks that her first task was completed.

Other towns fell, but instead of marching to seize Paris, it was decided to go to Rheims for the crowning of the king. There in the great cathedral Joan stood beside the Dauphin in her white armor and scarlet cape, holding her banner, and watched the archbishop anoint Charles and crown him. When it was over, she embraced his knees and wept. In the nine months since she had left Vaucouleurs, the salvation of France had been set in motion in a manner without parallel in history. The second of her tasks was completed. The third she would not live to see but within the next decade the English would be driven from France.

Instead of moving on to Paris, Charles ordered the army and Joan back to Gien. Later when an attack on Paris was finally initiated, it failed. The morale of the army collapsed and one by one Joan's friends drifted off. Finally she was left alone at the court and blamed for the defeat. The following May when a third move on Paris was underway, Joan learned from her voices that she would be taken prisoner, and on May 23 she was captured at six o'clock in the evening on a bridge before the village of Margny.

At first she was courageous, even happy, and twice tried to escape. Then the Burgundians turned her over to the English and Archbishop Cauchon of Beauvais, who hated her with a passion and wanted to burn her as a witch to discredit the coronation of Charles. Moved to a castle in Rouen, in fetters night and day, the agony began. Visitors, interrogators, and the curious came endlessly. Her jailers, brutal and insulting, forebore to assault her only for fear she was a witch. Denied Mass and the sacraments, a priest came to hear her confession while two scribes in an adjoining room listened and wrote down what she said.

A few days after her nineteenth birthday her trial on charges of heresy began before fifty clerical judges. It was illegal from the start. As she pointed out, the church had already examined her at Poitier and found her orthodox. Only a General Church Council now had a right to try her, but this fact was ignored. Questions of such theological intricacy were asked that even one of the judges protested. Her clear, intelligent answers only infuriated the others.

For weeks they badgered her to deny her visions and to confess to lies and witchcraft. She was threatened with torture, warned of damnation, and still no one came to the aid of this solitary girl. No offer of ransom arrived from the king. Her friends were silent. No faithful soldiers tried to rescue her. At last, exhausted, abandoned, afraid, she "submitted to the church"—in reality to her enemies—and denied her visions. Her head was shaved and, promised her removal to a church prison with a woman companion, she changed to female clothing. And nothing changed. A young English noble tried to rape her, her jailers beat her, and in a vision she was rebuked by her voices for betraying the truth.

Suddenly she knew it was not worth living if the price was to deny what she believed—her visions, her voices, her mission from God. Boldly she refuted the document she had signed in recanting, resumed her male attire (her only protection), and waited to die. Her saints had died for the same reason.

When they came to get her on the morning of May 30, 1431, she wept to think that her body, which at such cost she had kept undefiled, would by day's end be ashes. Dressed in a long garment and a miter-like cap lettered with "Heretic, Relapsed, Apostate, Idolator," they took her off in a cart guarded by eight hundred soldiers. Her judges were seated on three stands arranged around the pyre, some of them already filled with guilt and in tears for the evil of their deed.

In response to her request, an English soldier made her a cross of twigs and another held a crucifix on a stick for her to see. To the two priests who stood with her until the last, she said, "Hurry! Get down . . ." The pyre, unusually high so all could see, prevented the executioner from giving the customary *coup de grâce* to shorten her suffering and as the flames rose she cried, "Jesus, Jesus." An English soldier swore that he saw a white bird rise up out of the flames. He stood transfixed until his companions led him away.

June 1

Saint Justin Martyr
Died c. 165

S t. Justin, whose honorable title "the Martyr" has almost become a part of his name, was a gentile, possibly of Greek parentage, born in Samaria near the ancient biblical city of Sichem around the year 105. His parents were sufficiently well off to send him to school to learn public speaking, history, and poetry. Most of all he loved philosophy, the study of the meaning of life. And he examined all kinds of philosophies. First he studied the Stoics but his soul was "athirst for God" and they taught him nothing about God. Next, a peripatetic teacher (the term comes from Aristotle who taught his students while walking with them) disgusted him by being more interested in fees than philosophy. Then a celebrated Pythagorean told him that he must first know music, astronomy, and geometry. Alas, Justin was ignorant of these. At last he met a Platonist who said that he could lead him to the knowledge of God.

Deeply moved by this teaching, Justin went to the seashore to be alone to ponder the mystery of God, and one day walking by the sea he was followed by an old man. Stopping to speak, he unburdened himself of his desire and the old man told him of a teaching more noble and satisfying than any he had studied so far. It had been revealed to the Hebrews through the prophets and had reached its fulfillment in Jesus Christ, he said. He counseled Justin to pray in the name of Jesus for the gift of faith because knowledge alone would not bring it.

Young Justin saw that the beauty of this teaching explained how Christians were able to face cruel sufferings and even death for their Master, something which had often puzzled him and for which he had admired the saints and martyrs. He was about thirty years old when he was baptized, probably at Ephesus.

Nothing seemed so important to him then as to help others find the truth and the peace he had found. Up to this time, the early Christians had been mostly very simple, uneducated people, very secretive about their faith, never revealing what they did when they gathered together for their sacred rites for fear it might be mocked and profaned. But Justin spoke openly about their beliefs, their rituals and Eucharistic worship, and for the first time someone wrote as an apologist, a spokesman for the church.

It was in Rome where he stirred up the antagonism which led to his death. There he took part in a debate with Crescentius, a Cynic who held that virtue alone was the goal of life. Having revealed the man's ignorance of Christianity as well as his deliberate lies about it, Justin won the debate and incurred the man's wrath. It was probably Crescentius who reported Justin to the Roman prefect and caused him to be brought with his six companions, five men and one woman, to trial as "atheists"—in this instance meaning those who denied the gods of Rome.

The *Acts* of their trial is one of the earliest and most precious documents of Christianity and, in a carefully kept transcript of the trial, records Justin's testimony in answer to the questions of the prefect. Ordered to sacrifice to the Roman gods, Justin and his companions refused and were condemned to be scourged and beheaded. They died some time around the year A.D. 165.

Justin and his friends were lay people who died gladly because they believed that in Christ there is no death. Justin's were the earliest works explaining Christianity in a popular way. Three volumes survive, two of his *Apologia* and the *Dialogue with Trypho,* a work he wrote to explain the Christian religion to a friend who was a Jew.

Although the patron of no particular group, surely St. Justin Martyr is one in spirit with all the concerned young people who are today questioning life and religion, as he did, in an effort to find answers that ring true.

June 2

The Martyrs of Lyons
Died c. 177

The Christians martyred at Lyons in Gaul in the second century were from Greece and Asia Minor and had come with the traders from the Middle East when they brought their wares to Marseilles and up the Rhone as far as Lyons. With this commerce had come people, and those who were Christian were accompanied by their priests, not only to minister to the new settlement but to preach the Gospel in this city which was the farthest market and the largest city in the empire after Rome. How did they come to be martyred?

Although in Rome Christianity itself was considered a crime, suspects were not supposed to be ferreted out. Prosecution was to be instituted only when the existence of Christians came to public attention, presumably through popular denunciation. But this the populace was quite ready to provide and for a variety of reasons.

For example, Christians were not supposed to eat meat that had first been sacrificed to idols (Paul wrote of this in 1 Cor. 8). They often suspected that only sacrificial meat was available to them in the city shops. One can imagine the effect on pagan shopkeepers and their businesses if the Christians, who were becoming more and more numerous, refused to buy their meat.

Elsewhere in the Roman towns and cities, as the Christian population began to multiply, the pagan temples became deserted, public rituals were abandoned, and traders for whom the sacrificial offerings had been a means of livelihood became impoverished. Denunciations followed,

Christians were brought for official inquiry, commanded to recant and offer sacrifice to the gods, and if they would not, were condemned to death.

Ironically, the greatest persecutions were not under the worst of emperors but the best. Marcus Aurelius, a Stoic philosopher and a ruler of noble character under whom the martyrs of Lyons were killed, took his own religion very seriously. He placed much credence in the popular rites performed for the welfare of the state. Christians who refused to take part in them, who would practice only their own sacred rites, and only in secret, appeared to him as obstinate fanatics. After all, were they not also citizens of the state? That their secrecy was dictated by their fear that the Eucharist might be profaned, should their liturgy be public, was not understood, and their clandestine meetings merely seemed to confirm suspicions that they were truly "enemies of the state." When shock waves from the cruel persecutions under Marcus Aurelius began to radiate across the empire, they finally reached the Christian settlement at Lyons, and at Vienne sixteen miles away.

The letter that records the sufferings of the martyrs has been described as "the pearl of the Christian literature of the second century." It was addressed by friends and witnesses to the churches of Asia and Phrygia and is found in the works of the Christian historian Eusebius. It is the earliest document to give testimony to the existence in Gaul of an organized community of the Catholic Church.

At first, Christians were merely prohibited from attending the baths and places of business, but animosity grew and soon they could not appear in the open without suffering "insults, clamors, blows, hailings, plunderings, stonings and confinements and all that an infuriated mob is wont to employ against foes and enemies." Finally they were brought before the governor, were questioned and imprisoned, and as an example to others a group of them were selected for execution. Their slaves, frightened of being implicated along with their masters, falsely accused them of incest, all forms of sexual immorality, and cannabilism. In the end they were abandoned even by people who had been their friends and knew their innocence.

Among those who suffered most horribly was a little slave girl named Blandina. "Through her, Christ showed that those who in the eyes of men appear weak, ugly and contemptible, are treated by God with great honor because of their love for Him, which displays itself in power and not mere outward boastings. For a while we were all of us trembling and her earthly mistress [who was herself contending along with the martyrs] was in torment lest  Blandina, so frail in body, should not be strong enough to acknowledge her faith frankly. But the child was filled with such strength that the torturers, who followed one another in relays and tormented her from morning to night with every kind of device, acknowledged that they were beaten and had nothing more they could do to her." They could not understand how so pierced and battered a body still could breathe. Yet she seemed to draw life by constantly repeating: "I am a Christian and nothing wrong is done amongst us."

Pothinus, the bishop of Lyons, who was over ninety and, according to St. Irenaeus, had "spoken with those who knew the apostles," was dragged before the forum also, accused, beaten, scourged, and stoned. Asked the question, "Who is your God?" he replied, "If you are worthy, you will soon know."

Together with a fifteen-year-old boy named Ponticus and three young men, Blandina's martyrdom became an entertainment for the people. Thrown to ravenous beasts—who strangely enough did not touch her—scourged, burned, and tossed in a net to a bull, she was finally executed. Altogether forty-seven or forty-eight were martyred, although many more were punished.

The bodies of the martyrs were burned and their ashes thrown into the river, in order, the pagans said, "that they may not even have hope of a resurrection, in faith of which they introduce into our midst a certain strange and new-fangled cult, and despise dread torments, and are ready to go to their death, and that too with joy. Now let us see if they will rise again, and if their god can help them, and deliver them out of our hands."

Perhaps the marytrdoms to be endured by the young today are not so dramatic, but they call for heroism nevertheless. Peer pressure to become involved in drugs, drinking, sex; manipulation by a consumer society to be indulgent, insensitive, violent—these call for a degree of self-discipline and courage which is not far from the resistance and faith of the early Christians.

June 3

Saint Charles Lwanga and the Uganda Martyrs
Died 1886

The first Catholic missions to central Africa were established in 1879 by the White Fathers among the Baganda people of northern Uganda. They were blessed with some success under a friendly local ruler named Mtesa, but when a cruel and immoral man named Mwanga came into power things took a drastic turn. Angry at his

Christian adviser, Joseph Mkasa, who had reproached him for his sexual perversity and for the murder of an Anglican missionary and his caravan, Mwanga seized upon a trifling pretext and had Mkasa beheaded in November of 1885. This cruel act was intended to instill fear in the other Christians in his household, but to his astonishment it had the opposite effect. His servants seemed only to be more inspired than cowed by the death of their friend, and held even faster to their Christian faith.

In May of the following year, the storm burst when Mwanga called for one of his pages and learned that he had been taking instructions from another, a young boy named Denis Sebuggwawo. This meant that he would not consent to being used sexually by the king. In a rage, Mwanga called for Denis and had his throat pierced by a spear. Surrounding the royal compound with guards so that no one might escape, he ordered the war drums beaten to call the sorcerers and royal executioners.

Aware of what lay ahead, Charles Lwanga, the steward who had taken Mkasa's place and was in charge of the pages, baptized four of the catechumens, one a thirteen-year-old boy named Kizito whom he had saved repeatedly from the king. The next morning all the pages were brought before him and the Christians told to separate themselves from the rest. Led by Lwanga and Kizito, the oldest and the youngest, they did so—fifteen young men all under twenty-five years of age. They were joined by two others already under arrest and by two Christian soldiers. Asked by Mwanga if they determined to remain Christian, they replied, "Till death!" His angry reply was, "Then put them to death!"

In order to avoid an uprising among the people at the sight of so many young boys being executed, it was decided to take them to the village of Namugongo thirty-seven miles away. After an initial imprisonment, during which they were starved and beaten, the long march began with each of the boys in fetters and chains. Father Lourdel, the superior of the mission, wrote: "The little band passed within a few feet of me. I was so overcome that I had to support myself against the palisade. . . . Little Kizito was laughing and chattering. . . . I was not allowed to say a word to them and had to content myself with seeing on their faces the resignation, happiness and courage of their hearts. . . ." Three of the boys were killed on the journey because they were too weak to keep up.

When at last they reached Namugongo, they were put in bamboo cages, fettered to stakes in the ground, and for seven days wood was collected for the huge pyre being prepared for them. On Ascension Day, June 3, 1886, they were brought out, stripped of their clothing, and each one was wrapped in a reed mat and laid on the pyre. The chief executioner, unable to bear the sight of his own son being burned to death, killed him first with a blow to the head. Above the ritual chants of the executioners, the young martyrs of Uganda, piled high on an enormous bondfire, died calling out the name of Jesus and singing Christian hymns.

Other deaths followed, Anglicans as well as Roman Catholics, all of whom died for the beauty of Christian teaching as they had learned it from the Gospels, and in defiance of the wanton and perverted abuses of their mad king. Within a year, the number of Christians had grown from two hundred to five hundred, of catechumens from eight hundred to two thousand.

In our own time the blood of the Baganda has again drenched the soil of Uganda, this time at the hands of another mad king. May their blood which has flowed so tragically be the seed of a new and vigorous growth of Christianity not only for Africa but for the world.

June 3
Saint Kevin
Died 618

T here are so many Kevins in this world that even
though their patron does not have a universal feast, it
seems like a good idea to tell his story. How much is fact
and how much folklore no one knows, but legends com-
municate love and reverence and truth in their own
way—at least there is no doubt about the existence of St.
Kevin.

Said to have been of royal descent, Kevin was born in
Leinster at the Fort of the White Fountain, and was baptized by St. Cronan with a name which means "the well-
begotten." He was educated by monks, was ordained, and
lived in solitude in the woods for seven years until he was
finally persuaded to form a monastic settlement where his
disciples gathered around him. One story tells of an otter
that brought Kevin and his friends a salmon every day to
eat. One young man suggested that "a fine and splendid
glove could be made from the otter's skin"—and from that
day the otter was never seen again.

King Colman of Ui Faelain sent his infant son to be
raised by Kevin, and it is said that for want of cow's milk,
Kevin bade a doe with a faun to give half her milk to the

94 ·

child. When a mother wolf killed the doe, Kevin commanded her to take the doe's place, which she did, and gave the little prince wolf's milk for his nourishment.

At Glendalough, at St. Kevin's well, the local folk will show you a stone with two hollows in it on which, they say, St. Kevin rested his elbows when he was in prayer, and which were ever after filled with water.

St. Kevin's is a story of the power of loving relationships, the key to the peace of home and community and world—and even the company of the beasts. It would be fun to serve a salmon loaf on St. Kevin's day.

June 13

Saint Anthony of Padua
1195–1231

Perhaps the next generation will know St. Anthony of Padua, not as the sweet-faced saint who holds the Infant Jesus on a book and is the finder of lost articles, but as the fiery young Portuguese called the "hammer of heretics" and the "ark of the covenant." It would be a change he richly deserves.

Christened Ferdinand, he was born in Portugal of a noble family and at the age of fifteen joined the Canons

Regular of St. Augustine. Several years later he met five young Franciscan friars on their way to Morocco to preach Christ to the Moslems. There they were martyred, and the return of their bodies to Portugal for burial moved Anthony to seek entrance to their radical new order, to change his name, and to aspire to the missions himself.

Soon he too set off for Morocco but he became ill on the way and had to return. His ship was driven off course to Sicily from where he made his way to Assisi, and there he attended the last great gathering of Franciscans at which Francis himself was present. At its conclusion he was assigned to the priory at Forli to say Mass for the brothers and to serve in the kitchen.

At an ordination where no one was prepared to preach, Anthony was chosen to speak extemporaneously, and his sermon so astonished his hearers with its brilliance and theological wisdom that he was made preacher to the province of Romagna. The learned heretics of that area met their match in him at last, and soon Anthony's reputation was spread throughout all of Italy and France.

Wherever he went, people crowded the churches to hear him. Merchants closed their shops, and housewives stayed up all night in the pews waiting for him. When the churches could hold no more, they moved him out to the street. When the city squares overflowed, they took his platform to the hillsides. As many as forty thousand at one time went to hear this short, stocky, swarthy young Portuguese with the incredible voice who preached like a recording angel.

Called "the Wonder Worker," it was his sermons which worked most of the wonders, inflaming the hearts of sinners, reconciling enemies, converting heretics. But there were other marvels as well and two of many such stories, often thought of as legends, are attested to by witnesses.

At Rimini one time when Waldensian heretics, angry at

his charges against them, had marched off, Anthony was walking alone by the sea reflecting aloud on how often the fishes are mentioned in Scripture. Suddenly those who followed him noticed that fishes had gathered and were lifting their heads above water and appearing to listen.

Another story about St. Anthony and a mule was also occasioned by a dispute with heretics, this time the Albigensians of Toulouse. A man named Bonvillo argued publicly against the real presence in the Eucharist and demanded a sign of its proof. Anthony must bring the host to the square, he said, and display it before his mule. If the animal, having gone without food for three days, bowed to it before eating, Bonvillo would be convinced—and the mule did. Needless to say, St. Anthony is invoked as the protector of donkeys.

In addition to his preaching, Anthony was also known for his love of the poor. He denounced usury, persuaded the state to exempt from prison debtors who could pay with other possessions, and pleaded, although unsuccessfully, with a local duke of Padua for the release of captives.

He was only thirty-six when his health broke. Swollen with dropsy, he retired to solitude in a wood where he lived the last months of his life in a tree house built for him by his brothers. He died on June 13, 1231.

The representation of St. Anthony standing with the Christ Child in his arms dates from a seventeenth-century claim of a devotee who was said to have seen him with such an apparition.

It is a Franciscan custom to give out St. Anthony's bread on Tuesdays to honor his love for the poor. Families might bake their own St. Anthony's bread on his day, or any Tuesday, and make an offering to the poor in his honor.

June 21

Saint
Aloysius Gonzaga
1568–1591

A loysius Gonzaga was born in Lombardy in Italy in
1568, the eldest son of a family whose members
ranked with some of the greatest villains in Renaissance
history—the Visconti, the Sforzas, and the d'Estes. The
Gonzagas, however, balanced their reputation for wealth,
power, and debauchery with a real concern for other
things—such as agriculture and irrigation, denouncing usury, and from time to time by genuine explosions of faith
of which this son was their everlasting boast.

Aloysius's mother had high hopes that, like earlier illustrious members of the family, he would give his life to the
church. His father had an eye on the army, however, and
at the age of four, Aloysius was provided with a set of
miniature guns and mortar. A year later he was taken to
military camp where he took part in parades, walking at
the head of a platoon with a pike over his shoulder—and
once, to the general consternation, loading and firing a
field piece while the camp was at rest. When he also picked
up the barracks language, his tutor remonstrated with him
so severely that the little boy was filled with remorse and
until the end of his life called this period his "life of sin."

At seven, Aloysius experienced an intense burst of religious fervor which he considered afterwards to be his conversion. At this time he added to his daily prayers the Little Office and the seven penitential psalms, recited on the floor without a pillow for his knees—Renaissance palaces leaving much to be desired in the way of comforts. At nine, when he and his brother were sent to the ducal court at Florence, its atmosphere of "fraud, dagger, poison and lust," quickened his love for chastity and he vowed always to remain a virgin. Here he devised a regimen for himself which could only have been modeled after his reading—perhaps the Desert Fathers. Why else would a nine-year-old fear "lusting in his heart" after a woman? From then on, it was said, he would not raise his eyes in the presence of a woman, not even his mother, nor let his valet undress him.

From our present point of view this seems a bit precious, but if one takes a look at highly motivated children even now, such intensity is not that unfamiliar. Some twelve-year-olds swim 200 laps a day to train for the Olympic swim trials. Some ten-year-olds practice figure skating every morning from six to eight, and no one feels it amiss. As for his modesty, there is a classic state of pre-puberty when "Don't look!" is the admonishment of the child who, having had no sense of modesty in the earliest years, now wants to get dressed in the closet. Aloysius Gonzaga was probably not the prude he has been so often made to seem. He was like many children who are attracted to the high goal and pledge their hearts to its accomplishment. We cannot judge other cultures and attitudes by our own.

Two years later, living at the court of Mantua, he determined to forgo his right of succession in favor of the religious life. An attack of kidney disease left him debilitated for the rest of his life and gave him an excuse for not appearing in public. Now he spent his time in prayer and reading, and a book about the Jesuit fathers in India suggested to him the idea of entering the Society of Jesus. To prepare, he began to instruct poor boys in their religion and to practice the austerities of a monk. He fasted on bread and water, rose at midnight to pray, flogged himself, and never permitted a fire in his room—all this without a director.

His plans for the priesthood delighted his mother, but his father, who suspected a family plot to force him to give up gambling, flew into a rage. He had the boy whipped, but Aloysius did not change his mind. When finally the father gave his grudging consent still other relatives, churchmen, and diplomats sent Aloysius on royal visits and secular commissions hoping an exposure to such careers would attract him, but he was unmoved. Finally in November of 1585, at the age of eighteen, he became a Jesuit novice. Six weeks later his father died, a reformed man, quit of his luxuries and excesses and at peace with God.

Under the direction of St. Robert Bellarmine, Aloysius was now told to abandon his extravagant mortifications, to attend recreation with his companions, to eat more, to pray and meditate only at stated times, and he obeyed. He said that resisting the impulse to spend time in prayer was the greatest struggle of his life. Convinced that aristocrats were strangers to humility, he asked to serve in the kitchen where menial duties might break him of the habit of aristocratic privilege.

Because of his poor health, he finished his studies in Rome and there he delighted in a small room over a staircase with a tiny window opening on the roof. His belongings were a bed, a chair, and a stool for his books. Often he would become lost in contemplation in the presence of his companions.

In 1591 plague struck the city and the Jesuits opened a

hospital where Aloysius, by choice, performed the lowliest offices. Although nauseous from the fetid atmosphere, he fetched victims from the streets by carrying them on his back, and within a few months he was ill with the fever which would cause his death. In an ecstasy he perceived that he would die on the Feast of Corpus Christi, and exultantly cried out, "We are going!" He died at the age of twenty-three on June 21, 1591. It was the opinion of St. Robert Bellarmine that he had never committed a serious sin in his life.

Aloysius Gonzaga is a patron of youth and has always, unfortunately, been represented as a young cleric gazing soulfully at the crucifix or rapturously towards heaven, looking far from the kind of saint with whom today's young could identify. The only portrait of him from life—an excellent likeness, one suspects—shows him as a serious boy of about twelve, buttoned to the chin, wearing an ornate ruff, and obviously keeping his thoughts to himself.

Two rather trivial items give a better insight into his personality. First, on one occasion he was playing ball and his tutor asked, "What would you do if you were told that the end of the world and judgment were to come in a few minutes?" He replied, "I would go on playing ball." And second, he never signed himself Aloysius, but always Alouis or Luigi. It was the head of the family at the time of his canonization who insisted on Aloysius. A boy who was known as Luigi and who would trust God to accept him "as is" at the moment the world ended seems much easier to know.

June 22

Saint Paulinus
of Nola
353–431

Paulinus of Nola could hardly have wanted for more. He was born of a noble and wealthy family near Bordeaux in Gaul. He was intelligent, gifted, splendidly educated, and was admitted to the bar as a very young man. By the time he was in his late twenties, he had held a number of public offices which enabled him to travel widely, visit the family estates he had inherited in Italy, Spain, and Gaul, and acquire a host of highly placed and influential friends. He was an accomplished poet and a prodigious letter-writer (which is how we have such an excellent portrait of him and his friends); altogether a charming, well-liked, and admirable young man. In time he married a Spanish lady named Theresia, a Christian, and they retired to live a life of cultured leisure in Aquitaine. What more could a young man desire?

Then Paulinus discovered the pearl of great price. Influenced by the piety of his wife and the friendship of St. Delphinus, bishop of Bordeaux, he was drawn to the teachings of the Gospels and, at the age of thirty-four, in about the year 393, he and his brother were baptized.

102 ·

Several years later, Paulinus and Theresia, still childless, went to live in Spain on estates which had been part of her dowry. Here an infant son was born to them who died within a week, and in their frightful grief over his loss, they determined to change their lives. They sold most of their possessions, gave the money to the poor, adopted an austere manner of living, and devoted themselves to prayer, good works, and the pursuit of perfection.

This so endeared Paulinus to the people that they publicly called him to the priesthood and almost against his will he was ordained by the bishop of Barcelona on Christmas day, 390—although he was not even a deacon.

In spite of this tribute, Paulinus pursued a previous plan to live in Nola, a small town near Naples which was the site of the tomb of St. Felix of Nola to whom he had great devotion. Disposing of his properties in Aquitaine, which incurred the wrath of his relatives, he again distributed the money to the poor and moved on.

In Rome he was warmly welcomed by St. Ambrose and other friends, not including, however, Pope St. Siricius nor the Roman clergy, who seemed to resent more than a little the uncanonical nature of his ordination. St. Siricius wrote the earliest papal decretal extant requiring a number of interesting things, including that priests and deacons who were married should cease to cohabit with their wives, the earliest known enforcement of clerical celibacy by the Roman see. No wonder he didn't fancy Paulinus who, although he and his wife were voluntarily abstaining from marital relations, were living together.

Finally at Nola, he and Theresia took up residence in a long, two-storied building outside the walls of the town and once more he began to dispose of his local properties. With the proceeds he built a church, gave Nola a much needed aqueduct, and supported a host of tramps, poor debtors, and other unfortunates in the lower story of his home. On the second floor he housed a semimonastic establishment for himself and a few friends, with Theresia overseeing the household. Upon the death of the bishop of Nola, Paulinus was publicly called to that office, succeeded him, and was consecrated. He remained bishop of Nola until he died in 409.

St. Paulinus of Nola was a married man who became a priest and a bishop, and a wealthy man who became an ascetic and a benefactor of the poor. A learned man, he was a correspondent of St. Ambrose, St. Jerome, St. Augustine. A poet of renown, one of his finest verses is a nuptial poem written for the wedding of Julian, bishop of Eclanum and Ia. He sounds more like the fantasy Christian of the future than a figure in the early church, and that makes him an appropriate patron for today's Christians who are discovering a new relationship to the church, and are seeking to understand the Gospel in terms of new times.

Paulinus discovered that the man who gives away his life, his wealth, his security for Christ's sake only finds it. By divesting himself, his blessings, accomplishments, and enrichments multiplied. This man discovered that to follow Christ in all things can never be anything but gain.

June 24

The Birthday
of Saint John
the Baptist

S t. Luke tells us that Zachary and Elizabeth, the parents
of John the Baptist, were descendents of Aaron who,
with his sons, had been chosen long before to serve as
priests in the worship of the Lord (Ex. 28:1). By the time
John's story begins, the descendents of Aaron were so
numerous that the family was divided into twenty-four
sections. Zachary was from the section of Abia. Only at
Passover, the Feast of Weeks (Pentecost), and the Feast of
Tabernacles did the priests of this family still serve, and
they so outnumbered the roles available that for the rest of
the year those needed were chosen by lot. Each section
provided two priests, and each served one week. Since
there were as many as twenty thousand priests, it was a
rare privilege to be chosen to serve in the Temple, and an
honor that came only once in a lifetime to be chosen to
burn the incense before the morning and evening sacrifice
so the burnt offerings might rise to the Lord in a sweet-
smelling smoke.

Zachary, like any priest of his family, was overwhelmed
when this awesome call came to him. His fervent prayer

on this occasion included a humble reminder to the Lord that he and Elizabeth were childless. This was the heartache of their long life together, for among the Jews childlessness was considered a disgrace and was even cause for divorce. Zachary's prayer was interrupted by an angel announcing the coming of a son. Unable to speak, when he at last reappeared to the people, they knew instantly that "he must have seen a vision" (Lk. 1:5–25).

It has been a tradition in the church that when the little unborn John "leaped for joy" in his mother's womb on the occasion of the visitation of Mary, he was responding to a baptism of love and grace. Indeed, there is a charming painting in a chapel in southern France which shows John merrily playing a fiddle inside his mother at the approach of Mary. But we have the word of the Lord himself that this man whom he called the greatest of the prophets was nothing compared to even the least of those who followed him and were members of his kingdom (Lk. 7:28; Mt. 11:11).

Whether Mary stayed with her cousin until the birth of the child, Scripture does not tell us, but we do know that in Palestine the birth of a child was an occasion of great joy, especially if the child was a boy. When the time came, the friends and local musicians would gather, and when the birth was announced, if it was a boy, the musicians would break into music and song amid the loud rejoicing of family and neighbors. If it was a girl, the musicians went silently away, although even a girl would have been welcomed with delight by Elizabeth and Zachary who longed for a *child*—not just for a *boy*. On this occasion the rejoicing was double.

On the day of the child's circumcision and naming they went with their family and friends to the synagogue and, of course, everyone assumed he would be named Zachary for his father. To their surprise, Elizabeth insisted upon *John,* a name which is a short form of *Jehohanan* meaning *Jehovah's gift* or *God is gracious.* Astonished, the neighbors turned to Zachary who called for a slate and on it wrote: "John is his name." Then his tongue was loosed and he could speak. Everyone was filled with wonder and they said to each other, "What will this child turn out to be? Surely the hand of the Lord is upon him!" Zachary, filled with the Holy Spirit, sang out his great canticle of praise (Lk. 1:67–80).

The birthday of John the Baptist has been celebrated on the 24th of June for many centuries and the date was chosen because, according to the Gospel of Luke, John was six months older than Jesus. That it falls on the day when ancient pagan feasts celebrated the summer solstice, the longest day of the year, is a happy accident. The bonfires with which the druids honored the sun are an especially appropriate symbol of John the Baptist, the herald of the one who is called Sun of Justice and Light of the World. That the days begin to grow shorter after the Feast of St. John's birthday remind us that he said, "I must decrease that he may increase" (Jn. 3:30).

It has been a Christian custom all over the world to light bonfires and have picnics on St. John's Day. In Mexico and Puerto Rico, where he has been called "the saint of the waters" in remembrance of his baptizing, swimming and bathing are part of the festival.

St. John the Baptist is the patron of all those born on his day or who bear any of the many variations of his name, as well as of bird dealers, cutters, and tailors. He is prayed to for the protection of lambs ("Behold the Lamb of God" Jn. 1:29) and is invoked against spasms, convulsions, epilepsy, and hail.

Saint Elizabeth (Isabella) of Portugal
1271–1336

St. Elizabeth, or Isabella as she is known in Portugal, was a peacemaker from birth, a quality that was totally out of character with her family tradition. Her great-grandfather was the bloody emperor Frederick II (a cousin of Thomas Aquinas) and her grandfather, King Manfred of Sicily, was one of his bastard sons. Manfred was murdered by Charles of Anjou (son of St. Louis of France) and his naked body was paraded through the streets propped up on the back of a donkey. Hardly a proper pedigree for a saint!

Elizabeth was named for her great-aunt, St. Elizabeth of Hungary. Before her birth, her grandfather, King James of Aragon, had broken with her father, his son Peter, because the king had given half of Aragon to St. Louis, king of France. Then the king banished the family from court for criticizing his incestuous affairs, and it was only because he wanted to see this new little granddaughter that he made peace with them. As a doting grandfather, he took her to live with him.

They made a strange pair. King James, his first marriage null, had tired of his second wife Yolande, sister of St. Elizabeth of Hungary, and in 1246 had torn out the tongue of a Dominican bishop who took her part. Yolande died and the king, weary of his third marriage, had an affair with a lady named Berengeria. This earned him reproofs from three popes and St. Raymond of Pennafort. He finally reformed, sent Berengeria away, divided his kingdom between his sons, put on a Cistercian habit, and died. Pious tradition credits his angelic granddaughter with the conversion, but letters from three popes might have had more to do with it. This was the grandfather who called Elizabeth his pet and said she would be "the greatest and most illustrious woman to spring from the stock of Aragon." He was right.

At six, Elizabeth went back to live with her father, now Peter III of Aragon. The tales of her piety and virtue are so platitudinous that one might dismiss them as pious twaddle if they were not in fact all borne out. She loved goodness, prayer, the sacraments, self-denial, patience, and generosity to the poor all her life.

Barely twelve, her betrothal became a pawn in the complicated game of European politics. Edward I of England wanted her for his son, and Charles of Anjou (her grandfather's murderer) wanted her for his. In the end, King Peter gave her in marriage to Denis, the young king of Portugal; and since King Peter was said to have attributed the happiness of his realm to her youthful prayers, one wonders if he wanted to keep her nearby. One historian writes that in accepting Denis in obedience to her parents, Elizabeth "renounced her secret vow to give herself to God alone." Small wonder so many pious princesses preferred giving themselves to God; giving themselves in marriage was only a little less than slavery. But at least, if she could not live for God in the cloister, she could on the throne, and she did so very effectively. Exposure to her family's tangled affairs from the moment of her birth seems to have developed her gift for astuteness so that, combined with her commitment to peace and charity, she became a model Christian politician.

Denis of Portugal was a poet, a liberal, an intellectual, if a bastard's bastard. And he had been excommunicated. The illegitimate son of King Alfonso III, his father had repudiated his wife and married Beatrice Guzma, herself illegitimate, who was Denis's mother. Two months after Elizabeth had left her father's house, *he* was excommunicated and she found herself the wife of one excommunicated king and the daughter of another.

The marriage took place by proxy in Barcelona and was celebrated when she reached Portugal. Denis had arranged days and nights of plays, balls, and hunts, with jongleurs, troubadors, hawking, and bull-baiting as part of the entertainment. Then one day Elizabeth invited the poor of the neighborhood to join them. She gave them gifts, and for the rest of their honeymoon they were followed by flocks of beggars. Her young husband had admired her beauty, charm, and refinement. And he now discovered something about her heart.

By the time Elizabeth was nineteen, she was responsible for making peace between Denis and Pope Nicholas IV, and the removal of a papal interdict from Portugal. At twenty she bore her first child, Constance, and at twenty-one her second, Alfonso. She had no more, although Denis had nine more! That same year, in an effort to avoid civil war between Denis and his brother, she called a council whose arbitration the king rejected, so she made peace without him by deeding a portion of her own property over to the other family.

So richly did the country flourish during the reign of Denis and Elizabeth that theirs was called Portugal's Golden Age. The king organized agricultural villages and helped Elizabeth build the country's first agricultural college where orphan girls were trained to make good farmers' wives. On their wedding day each couple was provided with land from Elizabeth's immense estates. She also established a refuge for foundlings, shelters for poor travelers, a hospital, and a house for penitent women.

The king reclaimed sand dunes along the coasts by

planting them with pine forests, the seeds for which Elizabeth is said to have imported from France and delivered to him in her apron. Only once did she support her husband in war: when he was called to intervene during the wars of succession in Castile. But even then her love of peace prevailed and, together with the Queen Mother of Castile, she helped to bring about a treaty of settlement which had evaded the men for years.

Once she is said to have been unable to pay her workmen so she gave them roses which turned into money. One biographer calls it "the family miracle," but at least it has become the family legend. Like her great-aunt Elizabeth, she was said to have been waylaid by her husband one day when she was taking money to the poor. Intending to rebuke her for her outrageous raids on the treasury, he discovered not money in her apron but roses.

Denis's private life was a scandal. At first Elizabeth was deeply hurt and jealous, but with time she regained her peace and cared for his many bastard offspring as she felt the children of a royal father deserved. But the sorrow most difficult to bear was her husband's preference for his illegitimate son, Alfonso Sanchez, instead of her own. In time, the young heir determined to kill this half-brother, but fortunately his plan failed and Elizabeth helped him to escape. The king angrily banished Elizabeth from Lisbon and persuaded Pope John XXII to publish a bull absolving Portugal from recognizing the rights of its lawful heir.

As though her exile for Alfonso's sake were not enough, her son remained so busy about his never-ending schemes for rebellion that he had no time for his mother. So she now gave her entire time to the service of the poor, giving alms, visiting the sick, and including in her daily schedule the washing of thirteen lepers. One day, to overcome her repugnance, she kissed the wounds of one of them and he was healed. When eventually both the men of Coimbra and the officers of the court came to take her by force back to the capital, the king realized her innocence and recalled her to the throne.

Once again in Lisbon, Elizabeth was able to pacify her warring son, to persuade the pope to withdraw his bull, and for a while there was peace. But in 1323 father and son once again faced each other on the battlefield. Arrows and stones were flying when all at once, a mule at full gallop tore across the battlefield bearing the queen! Shamed, the king and his son were moved to tears by her heroism for them both and made their final reconciliation on the field of blood.

The king died a year later in her arms. Two days after, she took the habit of the Poor Clares and, although remaining the queen, she lived in their convent from that time on. Once more she was mediatrix in a war between her son, now king of Portugal, and her son-in-law, king of Castile. This last effort strained her failing health beyond recovery, and on her deathbed she summoned the two and charged them to rule justly and not to afflict their people with war.

A week later, dying, she called her daughter-in-law to bring a chair to her bedside for ". . . this lady." "What lady?" asked Queen Beatrice. "She is drawing near, in garments of white, and smiling," said Elizabeth. Smiling herself, she began to recite a prayer in honor of the Virgin, and died. It was July 8, 1336. She loved God and hated war, as her life bore witness.

Saint
Maria Goretti
1890–1902

Maria Goretti is a martyr because she died for a Christian virtue, but that is not why she is a saint. What makes a saint is how one lives, and at her canonization it was said: "Even if she had not been a martyr, she would still have been a saint, so holy was her everyday life." If her martyrdom served any purpose other than to determine the manner of her death, it was to spotlight a life so simple that we would not know her but for that awful violence.

She was born in 1890 in a village in the Apennines, the second child of a farm laborer, Luigi Goretti, and his wife, Assunta. Forced by poverty to leave their mountain home, they went to Rome with their children and all their belongings in an ox cart and settled in Ferriere, in the oppressive Pontine marshes outside the city. There Luigi found a neglected farm belonging to a local landholder and contracted with him to become its tenant farmer.

By the fall of their first year in Ferriere, Luigi had contracted the dread malaria of the region and one year later, in order to survive, he was forced to share work, profits, even room in his house with Giovanni Serenelli and his son Alessandro. In April of the following year, he died.

Desperate to survive, Assunta took Luigi's place in the fields, and Maria, at twelve, became the family's little mother—cooking, cleaning, mending, minding the babies. She was a slender little girl, modestly pretty with light chestnut hair and a tranquil, innocent face. In height she reached to Alessandro's shoulder. All her life had been lived in the atmosphere of her parents' piety and she had learned to accept both hardships and joys as coming from the hand of God. It was an attitude that sweetened sacrifices and disappointments with the knowledge that one could do all for Jesus and nothing would be wasted or meaningless. Maria's devotion to the Lord was unquestioning and total. He was the loving master who came to her in Holy Communion, whom she loved with all her heart, whom she wanted to please by being good. Her mother said that Maria in all her short life had never been disobedient.

Alessandro Serenelli, though a hard worker, quiet and withdrawn, was at eighteen a profoundly disturbed young man. His deranged mother had tried to drown him in a river at infancy and his brother Pietro had saved him. Another brother was in the insane asylum. Alessandro lived with Pietro until he was thirteen and then found work on the fishing vessels that sailed along the coast. For four years his companions were sailors, and his school the life of the ports that he shared with them—in all, that is, except their sexual adventures. In that respect, he kept to himself and spent most of his time reading, avidly and unselectively—books, magazines, newspapers, trash. For company he cut out pictures of girls and pasted them by his bunk. Assunta Goretti worried when she discovered romantic pictures pasted on the walls of his room, but with Luigi gone she was more than ever dependent upon the Serenellis and it seemed important to avoid disputes.

To Maria, Alessandro was like a big brother so she was totally unprepared for his physical advances—once when they were working in the fields, and a second time in the barn below their living quarters. When she darted from him terrified, he threatened that if she told her mother, he would kill her. Why should she resist? he wondered later. Plenty of girls got pregnant and got married. That's all he had in mind.

From that time on, she lived in fear. She could not tell her mother, who was already overburdened with worry and exhaustion, and now she feared living in the same house with Alessandro. She also feared for Alessandro's soul. How could he want to do such a sinful thing?

It was a sultry day in July and while Maria sat on the outside landing of the house in full view, mending, Alessandro returned to the house on a pretense. He pulled her into the kitchen and threatened her with the broad blade of a brush hook. She struggled fiercely. He stabbed her fourteen times, piercing her heart, her lungs, severing her intestines. The peasant women in their frantic effort to staunch the blood, poured vinegar and salt into her wounds. Later she remained conscious while surgeons at the hospital tried to suture them.

She lived for twenty-four hours, more concerned for her mother and where she would spend the night than for her own agony. She received Holy Communion, and was able to forgive Alessandro. "I forgive him and I want him with me in paradise." In terrible thirst, she cried out for water but the doctors could not permit her to have it. She died on July 6, 1902. Thousands of people filed past her casket in the hospital chapel.

Alessandro was arrested, tried, and condemned to thirty years in prison. At first surly and unrepentant, in his sixth year there he dreamed of Maria handing him a sheaf of fourteen lilies, one for each of her wounds, saying, "Alessandro, I forgive you, and one day you will be here with me." It marked his repentance and conversion and he served the balance of his sentence in the spirit of reparation. Returned to the world, he sought Assunta to beg her forgiveness and she took him to her heart. As long as she lived, she called him "her beloved son, her Alessandro."

Maria Goretti's story is not just a tale of a sexual crime. It is incomplete without Alessandro's repentance and Assunta's forgiveness. It is even more broadly a tale of the crimes of the wealthy and the powerful and the indifferent who produce and tolerate the poverty and injustice that afflict the poor. And such crimes still claim victims today in any community which cares more for money than people.

July 22

Saint Mary Magdalen
First Century

The saint whose feast is celebrated on July 22 in the liturgy of the Western church is a composite portrait of three people—Mary of Magdala from whom seven devils were driven (or who was possibly cured of epilepsy), the unnamed woman who anointed Jesus' head with perfume, and Mary, the sister of Martha and Lazarus. Modern scholars doubt that the three figures can be the same woman. Jerome, Ambrose, Augustine, Albert the Great, and Thomas Aquinas were undecided. But the popular conception of Mary Magdalen is a blend of the three stories. Matthew quotes Jesus as saying that the unknown woman's anointing (Mt. 26:13) of him would make her remembered all over the world wherever the Gospel is preached—and it has—and he called her Mary Magdalen.

The setting of the story is the house of Simon the leper, a Pharisee who once must have been both unclean and unwelcome in the community. But now he was healed and affluent and the host at a dinner at which Jesus was one of the guests. As they reclined at table, there entered from the outside a "woman of the city known as a sinner" (Lk. 7:37). She carried an alabaster jar of precious ointment, a beautifully fashioned amphora with its perfume sealed so that it could only be used if the jar were broken (Mk. 14:3–9). It was made from costly nard from the far-off Himalayas and its value was 300 denarii, equal to ten months' wages for a poor man.

Weeping, the woman bathed Jesus' feet with her tears, dried them with her hair and, breaking the jar, she anointed him with the perfume. For this she is forever the symbol of the sinner whose extravagant gesture marks the breaking away from an old life and the pouring out of self in the new.

She was condemned at once in all the familiar ways. First by Simon who had once been unclean and unwanted; then by the disciples for being wasteful and foolish, and finally by the other guests for making a scene.

Jesus was quick to respond. He pointed out to Simon that *he* had not even fulfilled the ordinary amenities due to any guest—the washing of feet, the hospitable kiss, the anointing of the head with oil. And he told him a parable of love and forgiveness.

He rebuked the disciples for failing to recognize the difference between the ongoing obligation to give to the poor and the celebration of a conversion. And to the others he said, "Leave her alone. She has done a beautiful thing to me" (Mk. 14:3–9). Turning to Mary, he confirmed her joy. "Your sins are forgiven. Your faith has saved you. Go in peace" (Lk. 7:48–50).

Mary Magdalen appears again in the Gospels with Mary, the mother of James and John, and Salome, as one of the women at the crucifixion "watching from afar" (Mk. 27:56). On that first Easter morning, after Peter and John had left, Mary began to weep, when she heard the angel speak to her. "Woman, why are you weeping?" She replied, "Because they have taken away my Lord and I do not know where they have laid him" (Jn. 20:1–10).

Turning, she saw a man wearing a hat whom she took to be the gardener, and she hurried to him. "Sir, if you have carried away his body, tell me where it is laid and I will take it." Only when Jesus turned and spoke her name did she realize who it was. Passionate even in her devotion, she flung her arms about him so that he had to gently disengage her. "Do not cling to me. Go and tell the brethren that you have seen me and that I am ascending to my Father. . . ." And hers was the privilege to say to the others, "I have seen the Lord" (Jn. 20:1–18). It is touching that the one thought of by everyone as the great sinner was the first to whom he showed himself.

There is a tradition within the Greek Orthodox Church that Mary Magdalen accompanied John to Ephesus where she died, and that her body was later taken to Constantinople. A groundless legend dating from the ninth century tells that she, together with Martha and Lazarus, sailed to the south of France, where she lived out her days as a hermit in a cave by the sea . Donatello's great woodcarving in the baptistry in Florence depicts her as an old woman with one tooth missing and wearing an animal skin. But the ghost of her beauty is still evident in the face, where a look of expectancy and the attitude of her two hands, like two moving flames, give a sense of her immolation of all that was fleshly—as though in the next moment the Spirit would sweep her up.

July 26

Saint Anne and Saint Joachim

There is nothing known with certainty about the parents of the Blessed Virgin, not even their names. The traditional story, familiar from legends, is found in the *Protevangelium of James* * which, according to one claim, is supposed to be authored by the "brother of the Lord," and by James the Younger according to another. Scholarly opinion holds that it could not have been written by either since it is dated no earlier than A.D. 150 and was not written in Hebrew or even by a Hebrew Christian. This is concluded from its ignorance of Palestinian geography and Jewish custom (the supposed expulsion of Joachim from the Temple for childlessness, and the upbringing of Mary in the Temple would both be impossible). That the author is a "brother of Jesus" is harmonized in the text by proposing him to be a son of Joseph by a previous marriage, which accounts for the tradition of an elderly Joseph whose role was to be a protector of Mary. It is interesting to know that St. Jerome disagreed with all this quite vehemently, holding that Jesus' "brothers" were merely cousins, and sharply attacking the whole piece.

Whoever he was, the author used sources from Chris-

---

* It has also been called *The Birth of Mary, The Revelation of James,* and *The Gospel of Pseudo-Matthew.*

tian tradition and from the Infancy Narratives of Matthew and Luke, as well as from the Jewish Scriptures—especially the storm of Samuel. This *Book of James,* as Origen called it, is barely fifteen pages long. The story of Anne, or Anna as she is called in Hebrew, and Joachim is a short beginning section which goes something like this.

Joachim was a rich man who yearly brought gifts to the Lord in Jerusalem, part to be used as sacrifice for sin, part as alms for the poor. Appearing at the Temple on one occasion, he was informed that because he was childless, his right to offer gifts was forfeited. Upon consulting the history of Israel, he found that indeed all the righteous did have children, and remembering that God blessed Abraham with a son in his old age, Joachim went off to the wilderness to pray. Without telling his wife Anna, he pitched his tent and vowed to stay forty days and forty nights without food and drink until the Lord answered his prayer.

In the meantime Anna mourned, thinking that now she was not only childless but a widow. Walking in her garden, she sat under a laurel tree and wept; even the birds of the air were fruitful, she mourned, and the fish, and the very earth itself from which water gushed forth merrily. She alone was barren, her womb closed.

Hearing her prayer, the Lord sent an angel, and when he announced that she would bear a child "who would be spoken of in all the world," Anna vowed to give such a child to the Lord. Now two messengers arrived to tell her that Joachim, returning, had had his own encounter with an angel who had revealed the same message to him. First Joachim went to the Temple to offer his gifts and then he went home to his wife.

In nine months Anna brought forth a daughter whom she named Mary. When the little one was six months old, Anna, vowing that her babe would not walk on the ground again until she had been taken to the Temple of the Lord, made a sanctuary in her bedroom where Mary dwelt and nothing common or unclean was permitted to pass through it. The undefiled daughters of the Hebrews were brought to care for and amuse her.

On the child's first birthday, Joachim made a great feast and invited the chief priest, the priests, the scribes, the elders, and the whole people of Israel. The priests blessed her and asked the Lord to give her "a name renowned forever among all generations." The chief priest prayed that she would be blessed with a "supreme and unsurpassable blessing," and Anna sang a song of praise to the Lord.

When the child was three, Joachim and Anna took her to the Temple of the Lord. Calling the undefiled daughters of Jerusalem and giving each a lamp, they placed Mary on the third step of the Temple and had the maidens lead her into the Temple so that she would not look back or turn back, lest her heart be enticed away.

So Mary lived in the Temple, "nurtured like a dove and receiving food from the hand of an angel." When she was twelve, a council of priests was called to discern what to do with her since she was now a woman. Praying to the Lord, the answer came that they were to assemble the widowers of the people, each of whom was to bring a rod and "to whosoever God gave a sign, his wife Mary would be." So heralds were sent out to spread the news throughout the country of Judea.

Hearing this, Joseph put down his axe and went to meet the other widowers, and together they went to the high priest who took their rods and entered the Temple to pray. Finishing his prayer, he returned their rods but there was no sign from the Lord until Joseph, the last to receive his rod, stepped forth. When a dove flew out of the rod and onto his head, the priest announced that his was the good fortune of receiving the virgin of the Lord under his care.

But Joseph was fearful that as the father of grown sons

and daughters, this marriage would make him a laughing stock, and he protested. However, when the chief priest reminded him of the punishment of Dathan, Abiram, and Kerah for the rebellion in the wilderness (Num. 16), Joseph took her under his care saying, "Mary, I have received you from the Temple of the Lord, but now I leave you in my house and go away to build my buildings. Afterwards, I will come again for you; for now, the Lord will watch over you."

Now it was resolved that a veil should be made for the Temple of the Lord. Seven virgins of the tribe of David were found and called for the task. But then the priest remembered Mary, that child of David pure before God, and he had the officers bring her to the Temple. The virgins cast lots and it fell to Mary that she should weave the Temple veil which would be made of gold, amiant, linen, and silk in colors of hyacinth, blue, scarlet, and pure purple. Mary took the threads to her house and wove them. This was at the time when Zachary was made dumb.

Thus goes the legend of Anna and Joachim and the origin of Mary. There follows, with some embellishment, the story of the Annunication, of Joseph's bewilderment, the angel's message, the journey to Bethlehem, and the slaughter of the innocents. It ends with Herod's soldiers seeking Zachary and demanding to know the whereabouts of the infant John. For refusing to tell them, the story goes, Zachary was murdered. The priests of the Temple, taking council to discover whom they should appoint in his stead to serve in the Temple, chose Simeon.

The Fathers of the Church rejected the use of such legends and it was not until the fourth century that the celebration of St. Anne's feast appeared in the Middle East. Crusaders returning to Europe brought back the legend and the name of St. Anne, and Jacobus de Voragine included her in his *Golden Legend* (1298). From that time, popular devotion to St. Anne has spread until now there are shrines to her all over the Christian world.

She is invoked as the patroness of grandparents, married women, and childless couples desiring to have children. She is called upon for fertility of the soil, for rain, and is famous as a healer of souls and bodies. Not the least of those who place themselves under her patronage are unmarried girls seeking husbands—based on the legend that she married three times, first Joachim, after his death Cleophas, and finally one Salomas. Inspired by her success, maidens in every country in Christendom have recited on her feast some version of that famous ditty: Dear St. Anne, please send me a man.

Whatever her name, it is certain that our Lady had a mother and it goes without saying that we should be grateful to her.

August 4

Saint John Vianney (The Curé d'Ars)
1786–1859

Someone has said that the Curé d'Ars looked like a sanctified Voltaire, and he did—but the likeness ended there. He was born in 1786, just before the French Revolution, of a prosperous farm family in Dardilly on the heights above Lyons. By the time he was four the Reign of Terror had closed the churches in France, and outlawed priests were coming to the quiet farmhouse in the middle of the night to say Mass.

As a boy, Jean had a little oratory in a hollow willow tree where he kept a carved wooden figure of Our Lady surrounded with flowers and mosses, and where he said his rosary. He loved to model little figures of priests from the clay he found on his father's land, and in processions with other children he was always "the curé."

Growing up, he cared for the poor and beggars with a prodigal generosity, bringing them home; washing off their dirt and vermin; providing clothes, food, and drink; and bedding them down in clean hay in the barn. Then he scrubbed the places in the kitchen where they had sat. As a boy, his father remembered how St. Benedict Joseph Labre had begged at their door and afterwards had written them a charming letter of thanks which became a family heirloom—until later when the curé gave it away.

Because he was needed to help on the farm, he had only a year of school, and not until he was sixteen and the churches were open again did he speak of his desire to be a priest. His father said No, but M. Balley, a neighboring pastor, persuaded him otherwise and Jean was allowed to study and live with him. His tuition was paid by a vocation fund because his father refused to help.

Intelligent but untaught, young Jean Vianney would have quit the whole venture had it not been for his saintly sponsor. Once a classmate was coaching him and became so exasperated with his slowness that he struck Jean—who then knelt to ask his forgiveness. Full of remorse, the young man embraced Jean and they became fast friends. His name was Matthew Loras, and years later as a missionary to America he would become bishop of Dubuque, the man for whom Loras College is named.

Having at last progressed far enough for confirmation and a recommendation for the priesthood, Jean was in sight of his goal when disaster struck. Napoleon's campaigns required troops and he was conscripted. He would have gone off to Spain had not the austerities he had practiced in imitation of M. Balley made him so ill that his company went off without him. He was left behind with instructions to catch up as soon as possible. He tried, but after miles on foot with a heavy pack, he collapsed in the woods of Forez, a haven of deserters, and was taken to hide in a farmhouse. Once, crouching under a load of hay when searchers came, he was pierced with a bayonet but he made no sound.

When finally deserters were pardoned on the occasion of Napoleon's marriage to Marie Louise of Austria, Jean hastened home and found his mother dying. Her last request was that he continue his studies. Her husband agreed, and at twenty-nine he was finally ordained and became curate to his beloved M. Balley. It was during the years with this revered mentor that he met Pauline Jaricot, foundress of the Society for the Propagation of the Faith, and acquired his lifelong devotion to St. Philomena. That anonymous little martyr was quite real, although her reputed name came from the words *Pax Tecum Filumena* (Peace to thee, dearly beloved) lettered on her small crypt, and the curé made her his patroness and credited her with many of the famous Ars cures.

When M. Balley died, Jean Vianney was given a parish of his own—although it was hardly a plum. Ars, a plain little village situated in a miasmic area twenty miles from his birthplace, had a church that was dirty and unkept, and people who were harsh and stupid. Seeing it for the first time, he resolved to love it despite its forbidding appearance, and he would spend the rest of his life doing so. The first thing he did was to send the elegant rectory furnishings, donated by Ars's lone noblewoman, back to her chateau with his thanks, and replaced them with the few pieces he had inherited from M. Balley. In an iron saucepan, he boiled his week's supply of potatoes, an iron skillet served for his pancakes. Other food sent by kindly neighbors was graciously accepted and immediately given to the poor. He ate sparingly all his life, forever battling the desire to eat more—especially fresh baked bread.

The faith at Ars was at such a low ebb that when the new curé came, he set out at once to make friends with the people and win their trust. He devised for himself an almost inhuman regimen of prayer and mortification for their conversion, including the use of a frightful discipline which left his walls splattered and his shirts stiff with blood. And he declared his own personal war on their dancing.

The Curé d'Ars's famous obsession with dancing has always been puzzling, considering that some of the saints thought it harmless, but apparently he had his reasons. Beyond the fact that his strongly Jansenistic spiritual reading condemned dancing as an occasion of sin, in Ars dancing was attended by so much wine and ribaldry that its consequences were alarming. The people of Ars did not do the stately gavotte or minuet but the bourreé, a polka-like step which, fueled by hearty drinking, degenerated into a rustic bacchanale after which the couples drifted off to the hedges—and nine months later saw the inevitable results. So the curé's concern was well-founded even if his theology was poor. He refused absolution to any girl who even watched dancing on the grounds that "she danced in her heart if not with her feet." He bribed the fiddler not to play at the village dances and so angered the young men that they covered his door with filth and even persuaded a local girl to shout under his window that he was the father of her bastard child. He did not succeed in ridding Ars entirely of dancing, but he put four taverns out of business, and wages long spent on wine were at last feeding wives and children. He mellowed in his old age, not toward sin but sinners, and it must be said that his tears and diatribes were effective for in time he converted his people to a love of virtue and innocent recreation which brought them much more peace of heart.

In 1824, he opened a school for the girls and orphans of the town, and it was during this year that the famous diabolical attacks appeared. Strange noises, voices shouting, sounds of engines, rats, rocks falling, the house trembling, his body moving off the bed, fire, filth—there is hardly a manifestation of such phenomena that the Curé d'Ars did not suffer. Whether evil incarnate or something else, the attacks were bizarre and terrible. They were witnessed by many persons, and they lasted to the end of his life. But he offered it all for his beloved parish, saying in the end that he and *"le Grappin,"* as he called the devil, had almost become friends.

At the time of his beatification, a celebrated graphologist analyzed his handwriting without knowing his identity, and wrote: "He has had to fight his passions to triumph over them. . . . What energy he has spent on this truggle! All that has become sublimated for him. . . . This handwriting shows an extremely violent nature but also a real saint, one of the most attractive possible. Since his genius has not been able to expand in the direction of the arts—literature, sculpture, painting, music—it has developed in his love for his neighbor, but a sublimated love."

He was small—five-foot-two—gentle and sweet, with piercing blue eyes and a pale face, hollow-cheeked and toothless. He had thick, straight hair, long at the back, which never became quite white. He was witty and sharp, astounding the clever and demolishing the snobbish, but always with kindness. He was a genius as well as a saint in the confessional, able to read thoughts and convert the most obdurate sinners. In time his fame spread all over France, bringing to Ars the famous and the infamous, among them Lacordaire, the great Dominican, and Blessed

Pierre-Julian Eymard, founder of the Blessed Sacrament Fathers. By train, ox cart, carriage, and on foot, they came to hear him preach and to line up in queues before dawn outside his confessional. There, finally, except for a few hours a day, his entire life was spent.

He suffered unmercifully from souvenir seekers snatching at his soutaine, his hair, his personal belongings, even bits of mortar from his house. He tolerated their adulation because it was unavoidable, and because of it he agonized in despair over his own salvation. He longed to run away from Ars and be a Trappist. He tried three times, and once he stayed away two weeks. One time a letter was circulatd by the other priests of the diocese protesting that M. Vianney had no background for all his spiritual directing, and when it got to him he signed it with a flourish.

It was always agony for him to rise before dawn and he never got used to it, or to the cold damp of winter and the even worse heat of the summer. He bore up under the stench of the crowds that passed through his confessional only by inhaling from a little flask of vinegar. When he preached it was in simple language that people could understand. He seemed to lose track of where he was, and the tears streamed down his cheeks as he gazed out over the crowd as though seeing Our Lord face to face.

He gave away all his belongings, even mortgaging things to go to people after his death. When he was made a canon, he sold the black velvet ermine-trimmed cape for fifty francs to give to the poor, and he was disappointed that the box awarding him the Medal of the Legion of Honor did not also contain a relic. He wore the medal only in his coffin. He multiplied wheat, wine, and dough; cured hopeless cripples; and saw Our Lady and spoke to her—and once two witnesses saw her speaking to him.

He died after three days of intense suffering in the terrible heat of early August. The villagers had thrown wet sheets over his house to try to cool it for him, while crowds wept loudly out in the yard. On his face was the smile of a child.It was August 4, 1859.

One of the tenderest stories he ever told was of an old villager who used to spend long hours kneeling before the Blessed Sacrament. The curé asked him one day what he did there, and was told: "Oh, I look at God and God looks at me." It describes the Curé d'Ars's whole life—looking at God looking at him.

August 7

Pope Saint Sixtus II
Died 258

August 10

Saint Lawrence
Died 258

St. Lawrence, after St. Stephen, is probably the most famous deacon of the early church, and his story and the story of Pope St. Sixtus II go together.

The emperor Valerian, who ruled from 253 to 258, had at one time been so well disposed to Christians that it was said his palace was almost a church. Kind and generous, no emperor showed the Christians more sympathy or made them more welcome than he for the first four years of his reign. But the empire began to be attacked on all its frontiers, and a high ranking official, Macrinus, a devotee of the old cults and superstitions, persuaded the emperor that the gods were angry at the tolerance he had shown their arch enemy, the Christian religion. So in 257 Valerian ordered the entire Christian community to recant.

At first, punishment by exile was the sentence for bishops and clergy who refused to sacrifice to the gods, but a year later harsher penalties were prescribed. Immediate death was the lot of both clergy and laity who refused to sacrifice, and nobles who admitted to being Christian lost their rank and property rights and were reduced to serfdom. It was during this second phase of Valerian's persecution in 258 that the story of Pope St. Sixtus and St. Lawrence is set.

The catacomb where Sixtus had customarily gathered the faithful for divine worship became too well known to the court so he changed their meeting place, but the precaution was in vain. Officers broke in as Sixtus was instructing the people, arrested him and his chief clerics and carried them off to the prefect. Lawrence was absent at the time and returned to find Sixtus gone. He hurried to where he was being kept under house arrest, and the scene is portrayed in one of Fra Angelico's most beautiful frescoes.

"Where are you going, father, without your son? Where are you going, O priest, without your deacon?" are the words Lawrence is supposed to have said. To which Sixtus replied, "My son, I am not abandoning you. Greater strife awaits you. Stop weeping, for you will follow me in three days." And giving to Lawrence what monies the church possessed, he bade him distribute it and whatever could be realized from the sale of the sacred vessels to the poor.

How much of the remaining story is true is open to question, but Christian piety has cherished details supplied by St. Ambrose, St. Augustine, and the poet Prudentius. Lawrence's legend is one of the best loved in all the lives of the saints.

When the prefect of Rome heard of these charities, the legend continues, he imagined that the Christians had great wealth and called Lawrence before him to demand that he turn over the treasures of the church to the emperor for his armies. Lawrence replied that the church was indeed rich and that he would gladly show its treasures but time was needed to collect them, so the prefect granted him three days. Lawrence went about the city seeking out all the poor who were supported by the church, and on the third day he gathered them together—the blind, the lame, the crippled, the lepers and orphans, the widows and maidens. Then he went to the prefect and invited him to come and see the "treasures" of the church.

Astonished and furious, the prefect shouted that the Roman Empire would not be mocked and that Lawrence would get his wish to die—but it would be by inches. He ordered the preparation of a great gridiron and had it placed over a bed of hot coals. Lawrence was stripped and slowly roasted on it. It was said that he neither felt the pain nor cried out, so great was his desire for Christ, and in time he smiled cheerfully at his persecutors and said, "You may turn me now, this side is done."

Prudentius accredits St. Lawrence with the death of idolatry in Rome and the conversion of that city. Several senators were supposedly converted on the spot by his heroic faith. They buried his body in the cemetery of Cyriaca on the Via Tiburtina, and Constantine built the first chapel in his honor there on the site of what is now one of the stational churches of Rome, St. Lawrence-outside-the-walls.

With that marvelous combination of devotion and utilitarianism which expresses itself in the popular choice of patrons, St. Lawrence is invoked against lumbago and fire, for the protection of vineyards, and as the patron of cooks and restaurateurs.

August 8

Saint Dominic
c. 1170–1221

St. Dominic was a Spaniard from Castile born about the year 1170 in Calaruega of the de Guzman and Aza families, minor nobles prominent in the reconquest of Spain from the Moors. His mother was Blessed Jane of Aza whose feast is also celebrated on this date and who, it is said, "passed on her beauty of both soul and body to this greatest of her children." Dominic was "fair-skinned with blond hair and a beard flecked with grey, beautiful eyes ever-smiling and joyous unless moved to pity by his neighbor's sufferings. He was slender and had long, beautiful hands and a sweet sonorous voice."

At seven, he went to live with an uncle, a parish priest, to learn reading, music, and the service of the altar. At fourteen, he moved on to school in Palencia for dialectics and the humanities. At twenty he studied theology, and he was ordained at twenty-five in the black and white habit of the Canons Regular, which would one day become the garb for his own Order of Preachers.

As a priest, he offered Mass daily—which was unusual at the time—lived austerely, went without wine for ten years, slept on the floor or the bare ground the rest of his life. He

loved prayer and study above all else, and his most precious possessions were his books, but even these he parted
with during a famine to buy food for the poor. "How can I
study on dead skins when living skins are starving and in
want?" he asked, referring to the parchment pages.

Nine years later, Dominic began the first of his lifelong
journeys—those first assignments on horseback to France,
Denmark, probably Sweden, and Rome. It was a time of
transition and ferment in Europe. He saw the church at its
worst and best, and discovered that many Catholics, including the clergy, were without a sound grasp of Christian
teaching and that heresy was rampant. One famous story
tells of a conversation with an innkeeper who had abandoned his faith and became an Albigensian. Dominic could
not keep silent and stayed up through the night, arguing
point by point with the man until at dawn he had brought
him back to the church.

From Rome, Dominic and his bishop were sent by Pope
Innocent III to join with the Cistercians who were strug-
gling to counter the effectiveness of the Albigensians at
Languedoc in southern France. This sect taught that all
matter was evil, denied the Incarnation, and rejected the
sacraments. They had as their leaders those they called the
perfecti, "the perfect," whose standards of purity and asceticism outshone by far the easy-going life-style of the
Cistercians. Seeing the common people flocking to follow
them, Dominic realized that nothing less than an equally
stringent self-discipline would do for those who hoped to
win them back.

He remained at Languedoc for ten years in spite of the
failure of the Cistercians, the death of his bishop companion, and the outbreak of war between the heretics and the
church. He preached, and he gathered about him a small
band of confreres, special preachers who would become
the nucleus of a new community. They would take vows of
poverty, go barefoot, walk everywhere; and above all they

would study, pray, and bring the fruits of their contemplation to the highways and byways, the inns and marketplaces. Wherever there was ignorance to be routed or the body of the wounded church to be healed, these preachers would go—and they would be called the Order of Preachers to describe their purpose.

During this time, he founded the first convent of Dominican nuns at Prouille, all converts from Albigensianism. To the three attempts to make him a bishop, his reply was a firm refusal. He was certain God had other work for him to do.

Twice Dominic journeyed to Rome before his new congregation was formally approved. The story is told that on the second occasion he dreamed of Our Lady pointing to two men who would help to save the world from perdition, one of whom he recognized as himself. The next day, while he was praying in a church, a ragged beggar approached and Dominic recognized him as the other figure in his dream. Thus Dominic and Francis of Assisi met and became beloved friends. To pledge their brotherhood, a legend tells, they exchanged cinctures, which is why the Franciscans wear the white cord and the Dominicans wear the black leather belt.

Gathering with his spiritual sons in 1217, he spoke to them of humility, distrust of self, and confidence in God. And he dispersed them to the four corners of Europe. "We must sow the seed, not hoard it," he said. Returning to Rome he established a large convent of nuns, sent a friar to make a foundation at the University of Paris, another at the University of Bologna, and over the years others in Poland, Scandinavia, Palestine, and in England at Canterbury, London, and Oxford. On one occasion he arrived in Bologna to discover the friary under construction far too stately and inconsistent with his idea of poverty, and he forbade the work to continue.

In 1221 as he lay dying at the age of fifty-two, he listed the bequests he left to his sons: "Have charity in your hearts, practise humility after the example of Jesus Christ, and make your treasure and riches out of real poverty." He died in another friar's bed because he had none of his own, wearing the friar's habit because he had no decent one to replace the habit he had worn for so long.

Before he was born, his mother had dreamed that she bore a dog in her womb and that it broke away from her with a burning torch in its mouth with which to set the world aflame. This dog became the symbol of the Dominican Order and from it came the pun which speaks of both its founder and his sons—the *Domini canes,* "the watch dogs of the Lord."

August 27

Saint Monica
c. 332–387

August 28

Saint Augustine
354–430

T he feast of St. Monica has been moved from May 4th to August 27th to precede the feast of her famous son Augustine, which is only fitting for a mother without whose prayers and tears he might not have turned out so well.

Monica was born in 332 of Christian parents, probably

Berbers, in Thagaste, a part of Africa which is now in Algeria, and her early training was in the hands of a strict but loving nurse. "Never drink between meals," she was counseled. "It is water you want now but when you become mistress of the cellar you will want wine, not water, and the habit will remain with you." Sure enough, when Monica was of an age to be sent to the cellar to draw wine for the family, she began to take occasional sips. They soon became cupfuls and one day during an argument a family slave called her a "winebibber." Ashamed, she vowed never to give in to the temptation again.

At seventeen, Monica's parents arranged a marriage of convenience for her to a forty-year-old violent-tempered pagan named, ironically, Patricius. It was not a happy marriage and Monica turned more and more to her religion for the strength and patience to bear his abuse, his criticism of her piety and generosity to the poor, and his anger at her refusal to join him in his dissolute ways. His only virtue, apparently, was that he did not beat her, and she pointed out to other complaining wives that often their sharp tongues were more to blame for the beatings they got than their spouses' ill tempers. For her perseverance, in the end she won not only her husband but her cantankerous mother-in-law who lived with them. He was baptized shortly before his death.

Three children were born to them, each enrolled as a catechumen but not baptized, as was the custom. Augustine, the eldest, was brilliantly clever and was sent by his parents to study, first at Madaura and then at Carthage. He spent most of his time after study, which he loved with a passion, pleasure-seeking with his friends in an atmosphere in which, he wrote later, "shameful love bubbled around me like boiling oil." A love affair with a young woman who lived with him begot a son. In addition, he became a Manichaean, embracing a heresy which held that

God was the eternal principal which caused all good, and matter the principal which caused all evil.

Monica discovered his way of life on his return home and was heartbroken. Thus began her prayers for his conversion, her tears, vigils and fasts, which would last seventeen years. She begged a local bishop to challenge him but the reply was, "Not yet, he is not ready and would not listen." But to comfort her he made his famous promise, "Surely the son of so many tears will not perish."

At first she refused to let Augustine stay in her home or eat at her table until she had a dream in which she was lamenting her son's loss when a radiant being bade her dry her eyes and said, "Your son is with you." Then she seemed to see Augustine at her side. When she told him this, he replied rather flippantly (although he always loved her and respected her faith) that they might stand together indeed, if she would give up her beliefs. Monica replied, "He did not say I was with you but that you were with me." Augustine felt years later that the experience was a divine inspiration.

In his twenties Augustine determined to leave the provinces and go to Rome, the center and capital of the world, to try his hand at teaching and rhetoric, since he was renowned for both. His mother and his faithful mistress tried to dissuade him, but when this failed Monica announced that she would go too. Deceiving her about the hour of their embarkation, Augustine left her at prayer in the seaport chapel and went without her.

Monica followed him and arrived to find that her son, disillusioned with Rome, had proceeded to Milan for a position as master of rhetoric. There he made the acquaintance of St. Ambrose, bishop of Milan, the most famous preacher of his day whom Augustine went to hear out of curiosity only to find himself strangely moved by the content of his sermons. When mother and son met again, she was delighted to find that although he was not yet a Christian, he was no longer a Manichaean.

Augustine was a great success in Milan and Monica was proud of his brilliance. Even so she prayed on, and was so often in the church that Ambrose noticed her. When he discovered who she was, he congratulated Augustine on having such a wonderful mother. Flattered, Augustine suddenly saw his mother in a new way, his love for her taking on a new warmth. Ambrose now became Monica's friend and spiritual advisor, and at his bidding she abandoned a number of devotional practices, among them the custom of taking offerings of food and wine to the tombs of the martyrs. It was too much like ancestor worship, he said, and it encouraged intemperance (local drunkards raiding the tombs?).

Augustine surrendered to the Lord at last and was baptized on Easter of the year 386 at the age of thirty-three. When Monica suggested that he might best make a suitable marriage and settle down, he said he preferred to remain celibate in the company of Christian friends, among them his young son Adeotas. On his way back to Thagaste to make a new life, he stopped at Ostia to see his mother and there took place the memorable scene with Monica about which he wrote so touchingly in his *Confessions*. Leaning on a window sill together gazing at the sky, Monica's conversation led him up to a vision of God such as he had never known before. She died not long after at the age of fifty-five, and the loss of her almost broke his heart.

Augustine closed her eyes, restrained his grief in public, but wept unabashedly in private "for a mother who for many years had wept for me, that I might live, O Lord, in thee. . . ." St. Monica is the patroness of wives and mothers, to be sure, but especially of all parents whose young are off today on scary adventures.

September 13

Saint John Chrysostom

c. 349–407

S t. John Chrysostom is known to most people as one of the Greek Fathers who stand solemnly in ikons, vested in scarlet capes over which hang great stoles ornamented with black Byzantine crosses. In reality, he was hardly that impressive a figure, being short of stature with a large head, an ascetic face, a pale sickly complexion—although he had a frank, energetic look. "A real spiderhead," to quote himself.

He was born around the year 349 at Antioch, a city where Peter had preached and where the word Christian was first used for followers of Christ. His father was an army officer who died soon after his birth, leaving his young widow with an infant daughter and son, the latter enormously gifted. He studied law and public speaking, at which he soon excelled, surpassing even his teacher at the university. At about the age of twenty-two he was baptized, a step which in the early church signified one's denunciation of the spirit of the world (and therefore was often reserved until late in life). After the death of his mother, he withdrew to a community of hermits in the

· 139

desert. He was a spoiled young aristocrat, and it is touching to read how worried he was about the kind of food he would eat, if he would have to do his own cooking, and "tackle rough work, fetch wood, carry water." But he plunged in, prayed, meditated, fasted, learned the Bible by heart, lived for two years in a cave, and was finally forced by ill health to return to the world. He was ordained at thirty-nine and became the official preacher of the bishop of Antioch.

Antioch needed such a preacher. Its climate was a mixture of paganism, Christianity, and heresy (Arianism). And its Christian population needed someone to teach, correct, encourage, inspire, chastise, and declaim. John was such a preacher. From his mouth there poured forth a "golden shower of words" (thus the name Chrysostom, meaning golden-mouthed) which bespoke his love and tenderness for the people and his rage for the vices of the time, not excepting those of the emperor and his court whom he excoriated, according to one commentator, in little less than shrieks. He gave hundreds of homilies and sermons, always standing within the sanctuary near the people, while scribes took down his words, which he later edited. One hundred sermons and 640 homilies still exist.

On prayer, he said: "Though you may not kneel or strike your breast, or raise your hands toward the heavens, if only your heart be warm, you have everything that is needed for true prayer. The wife weaving or working the spindle can raise her heart towards heaven in ardent prayer to the Almighty. The husband standing in the marketplace can also raise his heart towards the Lord. Even a slave, if busy and unable to go to Church because he is minding the oxen, can relieve his mind in prayer. God . . . is concerned with one thing alone: a pious mind and a pure soul."

In 397, John became archbishop of Constantinople. He

immediately cut down ecclesiastical expenses, used the money he saved for hospitals for the poor, deposed thirteen bishops for simony and licentiousness, castigated monks who spent their time at the court, and forbade ecclesiastics to continue using lay sisters for servants. He was censured for his mildness toward sinners, inviting them to repentance with the compassion of a most tender father while being equally inflexible toward the impenitent. Alas, added to these good deeds must be Chrysostom's six virulent sermons against the Jews, probably the most violent anti-Semitic utterances from any Christian in the history of the church. If, as has been held, in the end he regretted his angry diatribes, frightful damage had been done which reverberated through the Christian community for centuries.

Needless to say, he made enemies, especially among the mighty and the powerful—not the least of whom was Archbishop Theophilus of Alexandria and Empress Eudoxia herself, whom he accused of being "a new Herodias demanding the head of a new John." Several political-ecclesiastical plots later, he was arrested by the combined forces of church and court and exiled on the grounds of suspected heresy and resisting church authority.

Hurried off to the desolate town of Ceucusus, his influence became even more effective among the irate Christians he left behind. Infuriated, the emperor ordered John's further removal to the extreme desert of Pityus, and his treatment at the hands of his guards was so cruel that he died on the journey. His death gave rise to a schism in the church, not healed until his relics were returned to Constantinople thirty years later amid great pomp and the public penitence of the new emperor in the name of his guilty ancestors.

September 26

Saints Cosmas and Damian

c. 300

The twins Cosmas and Damian are the patrons of the medical profession. Of the little that is known of them, only these things seem certain: they were born in Arabia, studied and practiced medicine in Syria, and they served the people without taking fees. Called "the money-less ones" by the Eastern church, they treated everyone in the spirit of Jesus' admonition in Matthew 10:8: "Heal the sick, raise the dead, make the lepers clean, drive out demons. You have received without paying, so give without being paid."

Once, it is said, a matron named Palladia managed to come between these brothers. One day she offered them money, which they refused, and the next day she took Damian aside and begged him to accept a gift of money in the name of Christ. Damian, hesitant to reject a gift given in the sacred name, consented. Cosmas, learning of this, resolved that he could no longer collaborate with his brother. The misunderstanding was eventually settled however, apparently with the money returned to the matron.

In the meantime, because not only their healing of bodies but also of souls had endeared them to all the people, their fame spread far and wide and came to the ears of Lysius, governor of Cilicia. The time was probably during the reign of Diocletian, an emperor who at first had been tolerant of Christians, and whose wife and daughter were Christians. But he had gradually been influenced by those faithful to the old cults and had sent out an order to imperial officials to hunt down the Christians. Lysius summoned the two brothers to appear and accused them of emptying the temples of their suppliants—probably meaning the temple of Aesculapius, the god of healing, in whose sanctuaries afflicted people would sleep, awaiting a cure. He ordered them to offer sacrifice, and when they refused, he had them put to the torture and beheaded.

In time, their bodies were transported by the faithful to Cyr, and three centuries later the Christian Emperor Justinian I prayed to Cosmas and Damian to be cured of an affliction. On his recovery, which he attributed to their intercession, he enlarged and fortified the town of Cyr in their honor. His was not the only cure attributed these saints. Many more, among them pagan devotees at the temples of Aesculapius and Serapis, were said not only to have seen the twins in their dreams but to have received prescriptions for their maladies. In time, even Christians, adopting the pagan custom of sleeping in the temple of the healing gods, took to sleeping at the shrines of Cosmas and Damian.

Their so-called Acts are without foundation and were written in the classical tradition, telling of stones which turned in mid-air and killed the stoners; of arrows which turned and slew the archers; of trials by fire, water, and crucifixion. What is probably true is that their three brothers, Anthimus, Leotius, and Eupreprius, were martyred with them.

Through an error, there appeared at one time to be three pairs of twins named Cosmas and Damian: one in Arabia, one in Rome, and one pair who died peacefully of old age. In reality, they are all the same martyrs, their multiplication is a tribute to the enthusiasm of their devotees and the problems of keeping track of a martyrology

handed down by word of mouth among the faithful. Cosmas and Damian are two of the saints in the Canon of the
Mass, most famous for doing something for Christ—for
nothing.

September 27

Saint Vincent de Paul
1581–1660

The de Paul family were peasants not nobles, and their
illustrious third son determined, in later years when
he was surrounded by nobles, that no one should mistake
his origin. Thus he took to signing his name Depaul or,
more often, M. Vincent. He was born in the village of
Pouy in the Landes district of Gascony in southeastern
France. He spent his childhood herding his father's pigs
and sheep, probably on the tall stilts used by the shepherds
in the district at that time. He was bright, so they sent him
to school, and his ordination to the priesthood at the uncanonical age of twenty was irregular but not unusual. He
continued his studies and at twenty-two his principal ambi-
tion, he wrote, was to be comfortably situated.

A strange tale of capture by pirates, enslavement in
Tunisia, and escape with a renegade Franciscan comes
next. It is a mysterious episode about which M. Vincent

himself kept silent in his old age after destroying what letters he had ever written about it. Scholars are not yet quite sure if it was authentic or invented. Be that as it may, he arrived in Paris at the age of twenty-seven, a nice but not remarkable young priest searching for employment. Happily he met an influential and holy priest, one destined to become a cardinal, M. Pierre de Berullé, who took Vincent under his spiritual direction and found him a position in the household of Margaret of Valois.

Now Vincent began to lead a life of self-denial and prayer, and in time Père de Berullé joined him to the household of the de Gondi family. There he was tutor to their children and spiritual director to the sometimes tiresomely pious Madame de Gondi, through whose concern for the poor, however, he found his lifelong vocation.

He was called to attend a dying peasant on one of the de Gondi estates, and when he saw the spiritual and moral destitution of these people, due to the ignorance and laxity of the clergy, he resolved from that day on to be their advocate. He preached one Sunday in the village church about the plight of a family, all of whom were ill, only to discover later that the entire parish had thereupon taken them food, more than was needed so that much was wasted. He called a parish meeting and formed his first Confraternity of Charity, the purpose of which was for parishioners themselves to search out the needy and help them in the spirit of "Whatsoever you do to these, the least of my brethren, you do it to me." It was the first organized practical system for helping the poor. M. Vincent was forty years old.

He returned to Paris and from then to the end of his life worked ceaselessly for the destitute, the sick, the abandoned. He organized wealthy ladies of noble families, whose names read like the social register, into "Ladies of Charity," not only to give money but also to visit the horror-stricken hospitals and to form committees to look after the needs of prisoners, foundlings, and prostitutes. He became chaplain to the convicts left to rot in the Paris jails while waiting to be shipped to their sentences in Marseilles as galley slaves (although the story that he once took the place of one is not true).

He organized a band of priests to work exclusively with country people, to take simple vows, renounce ecclesiastical privilege, and live from a common fund. Thus the Congregation of the Missions (Vincentians) was born. With the help of Louise de Merillac (later Saint), he designed a program of spiritual and practical training for the hardy young women of the parish confraternities so they might become nurses, teachers, and household helpers, and care for the abandoned babies who were often sold to be mutilated and trained to beg. Working in prisons and hospitals with the victims of war and plague, he called them his "Daughters of Charity" and insisted that they wear secular clothing since at that time religious women were expected to remain in cloisters. They grew into the largest community of sisters in the world.

Former peasant and shepherd, Vincent de Paul became a friend of the rich and the powerful, a confidant of kings, spiritual director to saints and ecclesiastics. He was called to the death bed of Louis XIII and was an intimate friend of St. Francis de Sales, after whose death he became spiritual director to St. Jane Frances de Chantal. The qualities most characteristic of him were humility and sweetness, in spite of the fact that he had a bad temper and by nature was disposed to be impatient and irritable. A mystic, he kept his prayer life hidden (except that it was *all* prayer, as anyone could see), and he owned to only one spiritual phenomenon—seeing a globe of light rising to heaven when Jane de Chantal died.

He was small and square, a typical peasant, with a bulbous noise and the sweet smile of an old man who has lost his teeth. He dressed poorly and rose daily at four in the morning. He was irresistible to those who loved him, infuriating to those who did not, and for years he carefully walked the narrow path between the power games of the princes and the ecclesiastics in order to lobby (as we would say) for his beloved poor. It was said that when he read the Gospels aloud at Mass, a look of surprise and wonder would come over his face as though he were reading the story of Jesus for the first time. He died at eighty, the father and model of organized charity at its most human, most dedicated, most selfless. At the time his cause was being investigated, the fact that he used snuff seemed of major importance, enough for some investigators to have second thoughts—snuff, which St. Bernadette used on her doctor's orders.

September 30

Saint Jerome
c. 345–420

What is most intriguing about St. Jerome for modern Christians is that sentimental reverence has never been able to hide his defects, and if *this* man is a saint, then we come close to a kind of reality which few saint's stories have allowed us. Jerome was a man with a disposition so naturally irascible that not even a lifetime of asceticism refined it, a man whose title "Saint" has to be reckoned in spite of it by his passionate love for the church and the courage and labor with which he accomplished his incredible work, the translation of the Bible from the original Hebrew into Latin, called the Vulgate because it was in the common language of the people.

Jerome was an Italian, born in 345 at Stridon, a town in
the northeast of Italy above the boot near the Adriatic Sea.
His family was Christian, well-to-do, possibly servile in
origin but now free. Bright and ambitious, he was sent to
be educated in Rome at the age of twelve; he stayed until
he was twenty. An eager student, he delighted in the spec-
tacles and games and was as familiar with the fleshpots as
Augustine, which he later bitterly regretted. As he became
adept at Latin and Greek, he began the painstaking copy-
ing of the classics, which would later become one of the
most famous libraries in the world. He was baptized at
twenty after the catacombs had inspired in him a kind of
martyr worship and a severely ascetical spirituality.

Returning home, he and his friends set up a little monastic household in nearby Aquileia. It lasted for three years
and then came to an abrupt end, possibly through Jerome's
genius for getting into hot water. Setting out for
Jerusalem, the little band reached Antioch where the
deaths of two friends and a series of misfortunes for
Jerome determined his decision to go into the desert.

His five years in the desert was a period of alternately
unrelieved agony—the tedious solitude, the temptations
of the flesh, the crude stupidity of the other monks—and
rapturous delight. His only relief was to study, and there
in a cell that housed his books and his copyists (instead of
weaving mats, Jerome paid his way by having books copied
for others), he began to study what he called the "hissing"
and "gasping" of the Hebrew language. The desert years
produced his charming *Life of St. Paul the Hermit,* complete with centaurs, satyrs, and other marvels; his *Life of St.
Hilarion;* and endless letters. Among these was the famous
letter to Heliodorus in which he waxed eloquently on the
subject of leaving family, children, parents, all, for Christ
and the desert—so eloquently that some of the fashionable
ladies of Rome were induced to comply. In time, taking

off for the desert became such a fad that the church re-
proved it.

Finally in 382, disillusioned and disgusted—"Better to
live among wild beasts than among such Christians!"—
Jerome journeyed to Antioch where he was ordained
against his will (he probably never preached a sermon or
administered a single Eucharist), then to Constantinople,
and in 381 he was summoned to Rome to be secretary to
Pope Damasus who commissioned him to translate the
Bible.

Here, at first, he was enormously admired. His pale
ascetic face, his body gaunt with fasting, what people assumed to be his humility, his eloquence, won swarms of
followers and a popularity so universal as to openly name
him as the fittest successor to the chair of Peter. Alas, it
was not for long. His exaggerated enthusiasm for the
monastic life, his outrageous comments on marriage
(which he praised only because it produced virgins), his
acid pen with which he cauterized the corrupt clergy as
well as the corrupt rich and all those who disagreed with
him, had the usual effect. He would soon complain that
"They that hate me are as many as the hairs of my head!"

But lest his faults seem to sum up the man, it should be
said that with those whom he loved and who loved him he
was charming and tender. There was in Rome among the
aristocratic families an extraordinary exception to the
luxurious life of the rich in the household of the lady
Marcella. It was the first convent in Rome and among its
occupants was the great St. Paula and her daughters,
Blesilla, Paulina, and Eustochium. With them and their
friends, Jerome explored the Scriptures and discoursed on
the ascetical life. With the death of Damasus came the end
of Rome's tolerance of Jerome and, together with several
followers, he left to take up permanent residence in the
Holy Land, waiting at Antioch for Paula and others to join

them. Reaching Bethlehem they built three monasteries—two for the women, ruled by Paula; and one for the men, under Jerome.

Paula and Eustochium soon became first-rate Hebrew scholars and assistants to Jerome, and once again an old complaint was resurrected: What kind of man was this to make so much of women? (He had been accused, and vindicated, of having improper relations with Paula in Rome.) Jerome lashed out in reply. Had they never heard of Debora, Judith, Esther, of Sappho, Aspasia, Themistes, Cornelia, and the wife of Brutus? So deeply rooted was this prejudice against women that in the Middle Ages, copyists often erased his dedications to them in his books and substituted "Venerable brethren." Artists showed him removing the thorn from his legendary lion rather than working with these female companions of his choice. On the issue of equality of the sexes, and the respect due to the gifts and abilities of at least the women who were his friends, Jerome scores high.

The years in Bethlehem saw continued work on the Old Testament (Augustine protested it as futile: how could there be anything in the Hebrew which had not been discovered by so many other learned men?), voluminous correspondence, and books thorny with controversies and denunciations of everyone and anyone he considered to be heretical. Among them was the bitter feud with his former dear friend, Rufinus, over the teachings of Origen. But the most tragic of his mistakes was to side with the corrupt and vicious archbishop of Alexandria, Theophilus, against St. John Chrysostom, translating into Latin Theophilus's shameless pamphlets attacking the saint whose death he caused. Jerome, who did not even know John, who could call him "mad, pestilent, insane, tyrannical," seems here to be the victim of malicious misrepresentation and the strain and hysteria of a life of severe asceticism—and his own stubbornness.

When the barbarians sacked Rome, Jerome and his friends did their best to succor the refugees to Bethlehem. And he wrote on—letters, commentaries, and translations, the latter in words which would change our language. For all his harsh attitudes towards sex, the thirty-six years of his life spent in Bethlehem in the companionship of women were the most peaceful of all. He died September 30, 420. His hair had long been white, his forehead ploughed with wrinkles, his cheeks furrowed with many tears, his eyes weak, his whole appearance neglected and woebegone. It is probable that the young Paula closed his dying eyes and saw to his burial in a nearby cave, close by the grave of her grandmother.

October 1

Saint Thérèse of Lisieux
(Theresa of the Child Jesus)
1873–1897

Thérèse Martin was born on January 2, 1873, in Alençon, France, the youngest child of Louis Martin, a retired watchmaker of means, and his wife Zeli, who was a lace-maker. Both parents had been aspirants to the religious life, had been disappointed, and had determined to live holy lives in the world. They met, married, and brought forth nine children of whom five girls survived.

Thérèse was the family pet. She was pretty and lively and intelligent—and, her mother wrote, obstinate. Thérèse herself remembered very clearly what she considered to be her childhood faults of vanity and pride. Such as the time she pretended indifference at being dressed in long sleeves but pouted because she thought, "I should look much prettier with bare arms!"

As egocentric as all small children, she was quick to beg

forgiveness for her misdeeds. "Maman! I pushed Céline and slapped her! I'm sorry!" And of course forgiveness was forthcoming. But the slightest attempt to be naughty, affected, demanding, or moody was frowned upon by her family. One time M. Martin asked her for a kiss and she gave him the pert reply, "Come and get it for yourself!" He walked silently into the house, ignoring her, and only the reprimand of her sister sent her running after him with wails of contrition.

It was her parents', and later her sisters', understanding of the spiritual life and their love and awareness of her sensibilities that gave Thérèse such a keen grasp of Christian virtue even in her earliest years. They did not flatter her nor indicate that she was unusually pretty—which she was—with the result that she dismissed all subsequent flattery on that score as nonsense. They taught her to practice self-denial in little pleasures for love of Jesus, and were models of service and generosity to the poor. Family prayer, reading aloud, lessons in counting and the catechism filled her days, together with delightful hours of play, fishing with her father, picnics and feast day celebrations. A childhood surrounded by the love of parents and family formed in her a complete confidence and trust in the love of her heavenly Father and would later be the key to her powerful spiritual doctrine.

If there was a single quality most characteristic of Thérèse of Lisieux, it was her overwhelming desire for all, the best, the perfect. Once her older sister Léonie offered a little basket of toys and trinkets to Thérèse and Céline from which Céline chose a roll of brightly colored silk braid. Thérèse blithely said, "I'll have them all," and took the lot. Later she would write in her journal, "My God, I choose all. I won't be a saint by halves!"

When she was four her mother died and the family moved to Lisieux to be near relatives. As her older sisters entered the Carmelite convent one by one, the desire grew strong in Thérèse but her youth was an obstacle. Having asked permission to enter Carmel early, she was turned down by the local bishop so she precociously asked Pope Leo XIII during a papal audience in Rome: "Your Holiness, in honor of your jubilee year, please let me enter Carmel at fifteen?" Her bishop was furious, the pope replied that she would if it were the will of God, and in time she had her way. From the beginning, she astounded the nuns by her maturity and wisdom.

Asked by her superior (her sister) to write the story of her soul, she produced a journal meant only for the eyes of the nuns but which has become one of the great modern classics of the spiritual life. In it she reveals her "little way," one of perfect fidelity to the demands of duty and to the presence of God in the hidden life. She saw herself as one of the little flowers of the field (hence her title, the Little Flower) small and hardly noticed but as precious to its creator as those more splendid and colorful. She wrote: "With me, prayer is a lifting up of the heart, a look toward Heaven; a cry of gratitude and love uttered equally in sorrow and in joy. . . . I have not the courage to look through books for beautiful prayers. . . . I do as a child does who has not learnt to read—I just tell Our Lord all that I want and he understands."

Unable to shed her blood as a martyr for Christ, she accepted the small deaths of the daily routine. She learned to survive such innocuous sufferings as a sister splashing her with cold water in the laundry, one whose rosary-rattling in choir reduced her to a sweat of irritation until she vowed to listen for it as for the sweetest music—and the irritation ceased. She had a keen understanding of human nature and laughed at its weakness in herself and others. "If we make a clever remark at recreation and later hear someone repeat it as their own, do we not hasten to inform all that we were the one who had the thought first—as though the Holy Spirit, who sent the first idea, could not send another one."

By her twenty-third year, she was seriously ill with tuberculosis and the remainder of her life was the martyrdom she had desired. She finished the last pages of her manuscript, as she sat in a wheel chair in the convent garden, in pencil because she was too weak to use a pen.

"It is not because I have been preserved from mortal sin that I lift up my heart to God in love and trust. I feel that even if I had on my conscience every crime one could commit, I should lose nothing of my confidence; my heart broken with sorrow, I would throw myself into the arms of my Saviour. I know that he loves the prodigal son, I have heard his words to St. Mary Magdalene, to the woman taken in adultery, and to the woman of Samaria. No one could frighten me, for I know what to think of his mercy and his love." One sees again the little girl running into the house to ask for and to receive her father's forgiveness.

It was August of 1897 and she would die a month later on September 30. St. Thérèse of Lisieux was the child of a comfortable, middle-class family who lived the life of the spirit in the midst of affluence and security.

October 4

Saint Francis of Assisi
c. 1181–1226

F rancis of Assisi is probably better known for preaching to birds than for the harsh poverty he embraced in his passion to be like Christ, and most people might be more frightened than consoled to come face to face with love like his. But he was gentle with lukewarm lovers too, and to know him even a little is to begin to love God more—which he told his brothers was their only work in the world.

The story is told that his mother asked to be taken to the stable for the arrival of this child, and there he was born like the Lord he would love and serve. He was baptized Giovanni, but his father, returning from a journey to France, insisted he be named in honor of that lovely country (which was the birthplace of his mother), so he came to be called Francesco. When his schooling was over, Pietro Bernadone undertook to make his son into a cloth merchant like himself, but Francis was a much indulged young man and preferred to spend his time carousing. Biographers say it is mere sentiment to excuse the dissoluteness and vanity of Francis's youth, but he had the redeeming virtue of generosity. Once, after he had turned away a beggar from their shop, he was so filled with remorse that he ran after the man, and he never refused anyone again.

During the war between Assisi and Perugia, he was imprisoned and, lying ill for months, he reflected on the strange end to a journey meant to be full of glory. Released, he armed for war once more, intending to win full knighthood, but on the way out of the city he met a knight so poor that impulsively he gave him all his beautiful apparel. He returned more changed than ever, and later at a banquet when someone asked him, "What is wrong? Are you in love?" he replied, "Yes—and she is nobler, richer and more beautiful than any other." It was a hint of his growing attraction to that strange lady (Lady Poverty) he would make his bride, and who would give him the name, Il Poverello.

Going on pilgrimage to Rome to pray for enlightenment, he saw beggars who so touched him that he emptied his purse among them and, exchanging clothes with one, he sat by the door of St. Peter's, stinking and filthy, to know for the first time the hunger and humiliation of the poor.

At home again, one day in prayer he heard these words: "Francis, you must now learn to despise and hate what you have hitherto loved in the flesh, if you would understand my will. And once you have begun to do this, you will find that all that was bitter and hard becomes sweet and pleasant, and all that you thought of with terror and gloom will bring you happiness and peace." Not long after that he met a leper and to overcome his disgust he got off his horse, gave the man an alms and kissed him. From that moment all revulsion left him and he understood that in the poor and despised of the earth is to be found Christ.

The voice spoke again to him from a crucifix in the ruined Church of San Damiano. "Francis, don't you see that my house is falling down? Go and build it up." Hurrying home, he took a bale of cloth from his father's warehouse. He sold it and his horse in the market at Foligno, only to find that the priest at San Damiano would not take the money. But he allowed Francis to stay in the church. When his father arrived with a search party Francis fled to the woods. He reappeared a month later so dirty and unrecognizable that people pelted him with stones.

Furious that the civil authorities would not force Francis back to the family business, his father had him dragged before the bishop. There in the court of the bishop's palace, surrounded by the curious, Francis declared that he would from that time call no one but God his father, and indeed would return to Pietro Bernadone everything he had given him. Taking off his clothes, he handed them to his father and stood naked before the people until the bishop covered him with his own mantle. Years later he was asked what was the most painful time of his life and he said, "The affair with my father."

Now he was truly poor, "no gold, no silver, no scrip," free to imitate the Master who had no place to lay his head. There was nothing sentimental about Francis's embrace of poverty; it was his response to Jesus' call to trust God as a loving father. Francis believed God could be trusted and that if his life showed it, others could learn to trust him also.

Before long, others began to join him, selling their property and giving the proceeds to the poor, until soon there existed a small company of brothers. He wrote a rule but when he went to Rome for its approval, Innocent III refused on the grounds that it was too harsh. Later he dreamed that the Lateran basilica was falling down and one ragged little man alone was holding it up—Francis of Assisi. The next day he gave the rule his blessing. On another occasion in Rome, Francis met Dominic, who had also come for the approval of his rule and the two became fast friends. There is a tradition that the two founders exchanged cinctures, Dominic giving his white cord to Francis who gave his leather belt to Dominic.

Still living in huts and caves, his rapidly growing community needed a place to gather for Divine Office, and a local Benedictine abbot gave Francis a little church called the Portiuncula, or St. Mary of the Angels, in return for which he yearly sent the abbot a basketful of fish as rent. Still renouncing possessions, he said, "If we have possessions, we must have we ons to defend them, from which come quarrels and battles. . . ." In other words, money = property = weapons = war.

A young noblewoman named Clare heard Francis preach and ran away from home to follow his way. Cutting off her hair as a sign of her intent, Francis took her to the Benedictine convent where she was later joined by others and there came into being his Second Order for women, originally called the Clares. Another time when an entire town demanded membership *en masse,* he wrote a rule for lay people who wished to follow the spirit of poverty and peace in the world, and the Third Order was born.

And all the time Francis's life manifested the joy and faith and simplicity which fills the famous *Fioretti* ("Little Flowers") with its wonderful stories. No mere nature lover, Francis saw in nature's paradoxes and mysteries a revelation of the presence of God. If he marveled at the simplicity and obedience of the birds, fishes, rabbits, leverets, doves, the falcon who wakened him for Matins, the famous wolf of Gubbio who gave his pledge of peace to Francis and kept it, he also wept and did penance for the failure of God's noblest creatures—those "little less than the angels"—to praise him as well.

He loved music, missed playing the lute, and often as he walked along he would pick up a stick and pretend to be playing a violin. Once, preaching to Clare and her nuns, he broke into a little dance. All his life he had a sweet tooth and on one occasion addressed a crowd, "You see before you a sinner, one who has eaten cakes made with lard during Lent!" One wonders if they were expecting quite *that*. At Greccio one Christmas, he created the first crêche as a setting for Christmas Mass; at one of the priories he had a little garden plot for sweet-scented plants because ". . . in beautiful things he recognized Him who is supremely beautiful."

On his journey to the sultan of Morocco, hoping for martyrdom, he defied danger by walking through enemy lines to explain Christianity to the ruler. The sultan, while not converted, marveled at the simplicity and wisdom of this ragged little man. Ironically, the enemy who almost did demolish him was his brother in religion, Elias, who took over the leadership of the order, altered its direction, and in the end treated Francis as little more than a simpleton.

Francis hated money. He called it filthy, mammon, "flies." Once when an aspirant sold his property and gave the money to his relatives instead of the poor, he said to him harshly, "Begone, Brother Fly!"

And then there is the story of the stigmata. Removed as head of the order, he spent more and more time in prayer on Monte La Verna, a place given to him by a local noble. There he saw in a vision a seraph on a cross, and after he roused from his ecstasy, he discovered he was marked with the wounds of Christ. Only then would he wear woolen socks on his feet, a decent, whole habit, and even bandage his hands in an effort to keep the marks secret. The pain was cruel and in the end, weakened from so many years of austerity, discipline, cold, and exposure, his health began to fail altogether. In an attempt to cure the pain in his eyes, a local doctor cauterized his forehead with hot irons and, although his companions flinched from the smell and the sound of burning flesh, Francis saluted Sister Fire gaily and said he felt nothing.

Finally, as he lay dying, he asked to be taken back to Portiuncula. En route, his companions made a wide detour around Perugia, so afraid were they that those citizens might steal their saint. Home at last, as they gathered round him he sang, even though Elias rebuked it as unseeming on his death bed. At the end he asked to be laid naked on the naked earth, as he had stood naked that day in the bishop's court, stripped of all but the being given by God. He died on October 3, 1226. Two years later he was canonized.

Without exaggeration, it can be said that Francis of Assisi changed the Christian world. Like another Christ, he forced men to reexamine their understanding of the Gospels. Out of his brutal self-discipline and poverty, he taught all Christendom to trust the Lord when he says that the man who seems to die is the one who lives, the seed that falls into the ground and dies is the one that brings forth fruit. Francis is the patron of just about everybody.

October 15
Saint Teresa of Avila
1515–1582

Was there ever a wittier, more delightful saint than Teresa of Avila—or in the beginning a more reluctant postulant? Born in Avila in Castile on March 28, 1515, she was one of the twelve children of Don Alonso de Cepeda and his second wife Beatriz. As children she and her brother Roderigo used to pore over the lives of the saints and play at being hermits. Once, agreeing that the martyrs had won heaven very cheaply, they set out for Africa to be martyred, but on the way they were discovered by an uncle and sent home.

In her teens, in a thoroughly typical fashion, she outgrew her early fervor and gave much attention to her hair, her hands, clothes, ornaments, lotions and scents; indeed, her concern for her appearance would last till the end of her life. At the age of sixty-one, she would rebuke her portraitist touchingly, "God forgive you, Brother John, for making me so ugly!" She and Roderigo took to reading the popular romances which had been her mother's favorite books, those tales of chivalry, of knights and ladies, jousts and loves which would one day be mocked so effectively by Cervantes. She was never happy, she said, unless she had a new book.

Her mother died when she was fourteen, and her father, alarmed at her frivolity, sent her off to a convent school from which she was soon returned in failing health. Now she began to give serious thought to becoming a nun herself. She was afflicted with guilt for what she was convinced were the sins of her youth, and explained that it was the fear of hell rather than the love of God which motivated her. At least she could spend the rest of her life doing penance. When her father said she could enter the convent only after his death, she became more determined than ever, and one early morning she and her brother, Antonio this time, left home—he to go to the Dominicans, she to the Carmelites. Far from feeling the elation of most young aspirants, her distress was "so great that I do not think it will be greater when I die."

Once again she became ill and was reduced to a state of almost total paralysis, on one occasion even given up for dead. But eventually, having abandoned the barbarous doctoring of the time, she prayed to St. Joseph and he restored her health. But good health was not altogether a blessing for Teresa for now she fell in with the distractions of the life at the local Carmel. Having originally practiced a rule of simplicity, poverty, and austerity, the Carmelite convents in Spain had become more like hostels for single ladies who entered religion for want of a chance to marry. Visitors, fashions, gossip, journeys, all were part of the life—and Teresa, with her gifts of wit and charm, was soon caught up in it.

She began to neglect the practice of mental prayer which she had taught to her father who still practiced it faithfully. She convinced herself that this was an act of humility, that her unrecollected life made her unworthy to converse so familiarly with God—and then in 1553 she underwent a conversion. An image of Christ crucified so distressed her one day with the thought of how ill she had repaid his love that she vowed to cease all self-interest. From that day on, weariness, opposition, ill health never again interfered with her service of God.

Ignoring her health, which improved immediately, she plunged into a life of prayer and contemplation which abounded in mystical experiences, appearances, and consolations. At first she feared them to be demonic, but her confessor confirmed them and in time she realized that if the true spirit of Carmel was to be lived, reform was in order. She launched into a plan to return the order to its ancient rule.

A disturbed hornet's nest could not have reacted more angrily. She was attacked, vilified, opposed from all sides, but eventually her faith, her wisdom, her humility—indeed her charm and personality—won over her opponents, even the obdurate papal legate.

In the first of her many foundations, the strict rule was restored: poverty, supported only by alms in return for spinning and sewing; no begging; no meat except on feast days; no private property; all things in common; beds on wooden planks covered with straw; strict enclosure; never to be seen without veils covering their faces.

She received the perfect obedience of her nuns because she governed with love, and put a high premium on intelligence and good humor. "Heaven preserve me from sullen saints" she said. She wanted them lighthearted at their recreation, as befitted Christians who were not tied to the earth or to things by the smallest thread or possession. She provided castanets for their dancing on feast days, and once when they found her in ecstasy, gazing at the divine Child in her arms, singing and bowing to him, they joined her, dancing and dipping gracefully in the hallway with her.

She reached the heights of the mystical life, about which she wrote in her *Interior Mansions,* and enjoyed the most intimate discourse with Our Lord and his Blessed Mother. She was a friend and confidante of saints. St. Peter of Alcantara, whom she knew well before his death, appeared to her afterwards to counsel and console her. St. Francis Borgia was also her friend, and of course St. John of the Cross, whose restoration of the ancient rule to the fathers and brothers of Carmel she aided and abetted. Their writings on the mystical life won each of them the title of Doctor of the Church.

She traveled the dusty roads of Spain endlessly, opening new foundations, visiting others, conferring with the rich and the powerful, the poor and the humble. She counseled, encouraged, corrected, wrote endless letters as well as her spiritual treatises, all the while experiencing both the raptures and the darkness of the mystical life. Her works, practical and easily read, are filled with the most profound spiritual insight. They reveal a charming and witty woman in whose presence one feels quite comfortable. Her concerns were not only with the life of the soul, but she wrote as well of the toothache of one of her nuns, whether a convent wall should be built of clay or stone, of the quality of the pens she used, the proper tip to give a messenger, the kind of seal to put on letters, what material stockings should be made of, and a recipe for pastilles to cure colds.

She was famous for her wry sense of humor. A sister who signed her letter as one "no better than dung," received a jaunty reply hoping that her humility was more than a matter of words. Criticized by a shocked visitor when she was found eating a partridge someone had sent, Teresa commented, "There is a time for partridge and a time for penance!" As for loving, she said she could be bribed with a sardine, so defenceless was she against affection. And, of course, there is the most famous story of all about the time her saddle slipped and she found herself head down under the belly of her donkey as she crossed a stream. Complaining to the Lord of his treatment, she heard him reply, "Teresa, whom the Lord loves, he chastises. This is how I treat all my friends." Her tart reply was, "No wonder you have so few!"

In her old age she was worn and ugly, her skin the color of earth, her teeth blackened, stiff hairs sprouting from the three moles which had once lent such piquant charm to her face. But as she lay dying, the wrinkles fell away, the skin grew translucent, and her beauty returned as though her soul had at last become visible. On October 4, 1582, she left life saying as they brought her the Eucharist, "My Saviour, it is time that I set out. . . . Let us go."

October 17

Saint Ignatius of Antioch
c. 110

St. Ignatius, third bishop of Antioch, was probably born about the time of the passion and resurrection of Jesus, was probably a convert, and that is all that is known of his early history. A Syrian, he had faithfully shepherded his flock for forty years when new local persecutions were initiated against the Christians and he was arrested and shipped to Rome to be devoured by wild beasts in the amphitheatre, where prominent and venerable victims were always a great attraction.

He was put aboard a ship with two companions under the guard of ten soldiers who were so brutal that, he wrote, they were like ten leopards. "It was like fighting with wild beasts on land and sea by day and night, who only grew worse when they were treated kindly." From Antioch, the ship followed the coast of Asia Minor to Pamphylia, where they made their way overland through a number of cities with Christian communities which, happily, gave Ignatius an opportunity to meet the people of the nearby churches who came in crowds with their priests and bishops to ask his blessing.

It was to these churches that he wrote his seven famous letters which offer one of the rare firsthand records of this early period. The first three, to Ephesus, Magnesia, and Tralles, were composed while he and his captors were waiting for a vessel to take them to Smyrna; and to the Romans he addressed a fourth, pleading that they not interfere through their political connections with the carrying out of his sentence, thus cheating him of his martyrdom. Some of his friends had already traveled to Rome by a shorter route for this very purpose. His ardent entreaty is one of the most famous passages in the writings of the early church, and its impassioned cry for martyrdom was new to Christianity, marking an influence which—while noble in Ignatius, and in others who spoke of being "in love" with their violent end—would in time see something close to a cult of marytrdom develop, which the church later found it necessary to restrain and reprove.

He wrote: "I fear your charity lest it prejudice me. . . . I shall never have another such opportunity of attaining unto my Lord. . . . Therefore you cannot do me a greater favor than suffer me to be poured out as a libation to God whilst the altar is ready. . . . Only pray for me that God may give me grace within as well as without, not only to say it but desire it, that I may not only be called but be found Christian. . . . Suffer me to be the food of wild beasts through whom I may attain unto God. I am God's grain and I am to be ground by the teeth of wild beasts that

I may be found the pure bread of Christ. Rather, entice the beasts to become my sepulchre that they may leave nothing of my body, that when I am dead I may not be troublesome to any man." He is concerned lest his burial be a nuisance to his friends.

His guards were in a hurry to reach Rome in time, apparently for some particular anniversary and its accompanying games, and Ignatius was as eager as they, but the final details of the journey are not known. The so-called Acts of his martyrdom are spurious, the Roman Christians having left no account of his death, and all that is known is that he died on October 17 under the claws and teeth of lions or tigers in the great Flavian amphitheatre—an entertainment for the emperor Trajan and his people. His death was as unrecorded as that of the apostles before him.

The last three letters of St. Ignatius were to the churches at Philadelphia and Smyrna, and to his young bishop friend, St. Polycarp. He urges them to look after widows, hold more frequent meetings, not to despise slaves, to encourage faithfulness and humility in married persons and celibates alike, and to warn the celibates not to pride themselves over the bishops who are perhaps married. The letters were written less than one hundred years after the Ascension of Jesus. Ignatius is the first writer outside of the New Testament to stress the virgin birth. He speaks of the Trinity, and of the Eucharist as "the flesh of Christ" and the "medicine of immortality." He was the first to use the word Catholic for the Christian churches, as his predecessor, St. Evodius, was the first to use the word Christian for a follower of Christ. Some 1,400 years later a young Spanish soldier would undergo a conversion, dedicate his life to God, and, after reading the story of Ignatius of Antioch, change his name from Inigo to Ignatius—of Loyola.

If his letter to the Ephesians were not dated A.D. 110,

one might think it was written today: "And for the rest of men pray unceasingly, for there is in them hope of repentance that they may attain unto God. Suffer them therefore to be instructed by the example of your works. In the face of their outbursts of wrath, be meek; in the face of their boastful words, be humble; meet their revilings with prayers; where they are in error, be steadfast in the faith; in the face of their fury, be gentle. Be not eager to retaliate upon them. Let our forbearance prove us their brothers."

November 3

Saint Martin de Porres
1579–1639

St. Martin de Porres was born in Lima less than fifty years after the conquest of Peru. His father was Juan de Porres, a Spanish nobleman who came to the new world in search of fortune. His mother was a beautiful black freed woman by whom Juan had two illegitimate children. Disappointed that they inherited their mother's color and features, Juan supported them but, except for one short period of time, left them in the care of their mother.

Even from his early childhood, Martin seemed drawn to the needs of the poor. Often when he was sent to the market, in spite of his mother's warnings he would give away either the money or his purchases to anyone needy he met on the way. At twelve, he apprenticed himself to a barber where he learned not only how to cut hair but also to do minor surgery, set bones, let blood, allay fevers, and apply poultices. He showed such a special gift for the work that at fifteen, when he asked to enter the Order of Preachers as a lay brother, the Dominican fathers were delighted to have an applicant already known for his skill as well as his piety.

As a lay brother Martin did the lowest tasks, to the great displeasure of his father who considered his noble origin merited the priesthood or at least the professed brotherhood. But Martin's choice was deliberate. It would keep him from the esteem and temptations that go with roles in higher places.

He worked unceasingly, slept little and wherever he happened to be—in the refectory on a table or the floor, or on the catafalque in the chapter room on which bodies were laid for funerals. Long hours of prayer, service, obedience, and harsh mortifications were the program he set for himself, and supernatural favors became so frequent that he could no longer hide them. Often he was discovered in ecstasy near the altar, surrounded by light and gazing at the crucifix. Frequently light shone beneath the door of his cell and he would be found prostrate on the floor in prayer or elevated in the air. Once his foot caught in the hood of a young friar who had entered the door to look for him. Such phenomena became so ordinary that the porter once commented, "You will soon learn not to be astonished at Brother Martin's heavenly favors." But there were others more ready to accuse him of hypocrisy, quackery, and being a fake—criticisms he always welcomed as good for his soul.

He was appointed infirmarian and cared not only for the sick of the order but for people from all over Lima until such crowds came that the convent of the Holy Rosary became a forerunner of the modern medical clinic. His ability as a healer was a source of embarrassment to him and he often disavowed it. One time he bade a desperately ill woman whom he had just cured to eat an apple, and then credited the apple with her cure.

One of the paradoxes of the times was that ruthless conquerors and fortune hunters, having amassed great fortunes, tried to balance their rapacity with extravagant donations of gold for the poor. In the city of Lima, the principal recipient of such monies was Brother Martin, who could be trusted to spend every penny of it honestly. It was said that he collected the equivalent of $2,000 a week for food, clothing, medicines, and shelter, and dispensed it indefatigably.

For months, every other day he walked under the scorching sun on unpaved dusty roads to carry food and clothes to Callao, a seaport five miles away where soldiers in a garrison were without even the barest essentials for living. Anguished over the plight of abandoned children who roamed the streets of Lima, hungry, shelterless, prey to all kinds of evils, he conceived a plan to build a hostel and school for them. When he at last won the approval of the viceroy and the archbishop, a wealthy chemist donated 200,000 pesos to complete the drive for funds for the Orphange of the Holy Cross, which still exists today.

And there was his way with animals, for which he is so famous. Mice frequently nibbled the vestments in the priory sacristy, and on one occasion after traps had been set and one was caught, Martin freed it with an admonition. "Go along, little brother, and tell your companions not to do any more harm. Let them vacate this holy monastery and go back to the garden, and I will bring your food there each day." To the astonishment of everyone, rats and mice went flocking from the monastery and never again came closer than the garden where Martin fed them daily.

Endless such events were witnessed—a mule rescued from a pit, a raging bull quieted in the city square, a dying dog restored to life, a mouse sharing food with a dog and a cat, a hawk whose broken leg was healed. He was equally known for his planting of herbs and flowers for the use of the friars, and olive trees on the barren hills above the city for the poor so they would not have to steal from the orchards.

He rose each morning at four o'clock to greet the dawn in honor of Mary, after an ancient custom, and she frequently appeared to him carrying her Holy Child, spoke with him, and interceded for his sick poor.

Innumerable witnesses swore to his bilocation in foreign lands—the Philippines, Algeria, France, China—and to his ability to cover distances with the speed of light, which earned for him the name "the flying Brother." Among his closest friends were St. Rose of Lima and Blessed John Masias, another Dominican lay brother at another convent in Lima. He died at sixty, this man who considered himself "only a poor mulatto," and he was carried to his grave by prelates and noblemen.

Saint Martin
of Tours
c. 316–397

T he feast of St. Martin of Tours falls on what used to
be Veterans' Day, and there could be no more appropriate patron for such a celebration than this soldier-
peacemaker of the fourth century. He was born of pagan
parents around 316 in Pannonia, in what is now Hungary,
his father was a superior officer of the Roman legion who
had risen from the ranks.

Early in Martin's childhood, they moved to Pavia, in
Italy, where he was drawn to the teaching of Christ. The
story is told that as a boy, taking refuge in a church during
a storm, he heard a bishop speak to a group of catechumens about Jesus, and he joined them. He determined to
become a hermit but his father and the state had other
plans. Universal military training was mandatory for the
sons of officers, and both his father's anger at Martin's new
religious bent and the law of the empire prevailed.

He was chosen for the elite cavalry corps of the imperial
guard, officers who were not supposed to fight save in the
emperor's presence, and whose dazzling uniform included
gleaming armor and a great white cloak lined with

lambskin. As an officer, Martin was entitled to two horses, double rations, and a servant, but to the amusement of the garrison, he reversed the roles. He served his servant even to cleaning his shoes. He ate the poorest of food and gave away what he did not need. And he neither drank nor mixed with women; instead he prayed and read and visited the sick. In the army Martin not only remained an aspiring Christian but became a better one.

Now comes the most famous story of all about Martin of Tours. He was eighteen and quartered in Amiens during a severe winter. One day, after making the rounds, he was about to reenter the city gate when he saw a naked beggar shivering on the roadside. He took his sword, rent the beautiful cloak in half and gave part to the beggar, wrapping himself in the remainder. That night in a dream he saw Christ as the beggar, wearing the half-cloak, saying: "Look, Martin has given me half his cloak and he is not even baptized!" His biographer writes, "He flew to be baptized."

By the time Martin's corps was called into battle, he had already asked to be released from the army to become a monk. Standing before Constantine II to receive the customary money paid to soldiers before battle, he stated that he could not take it because he could not go into battle and kill. Enraged, the emperor said he *would* go, but with a sword at his back, and Martin agreed to go—but unarmed. He was cast into prison for the night where he prayed until dawn, and to the astonishment of everyone, envoys came from the enemy to ask for peace.

Now twenty-five, Martin sought out the hermit bishop of Poitiers, St. Hilary, to be his mentor. Refusing ordination, he studied, took minor orders, and then felt called to cross the Alps to see his parents again. He converted his mother but not his father, and as he was about to return, he ran afoul of the Arians in the vicinity. He preached against them so eloquently that he was beaten and driven away. Reaching Milan he took refuge on an island until Hilary, temporarily exiled, was permitted to return to Poitiers, and there Martin once again joined him. He lived for ten years in a hut, first as a hermit, then, joined by others, founding the first monastic community in Gaul. Eventually, he accepted ordination.

In the year 371, the bishop of Tours died and his people set about to choose another bishop. Martin, famous for his holiness and love for souls, was their choice, much against the judgment of some of the more worldly clergy who objected that he was too unkempt and shabby, with hardly a bishop's style. The people replied that they wanted a holy bishop, not a stylish one, and were determined to have Martin. Horrified, he refused, and the people, resorting to a ruse, captured him and forcibly made him bishop of Tours. A charming legend tells that Martin hid from them between two farm buildings, but his pet goose followed and honked at him and gave his hiding place away—which explains the presence of a goose in so many representations of Martin of Tours.

Martin took his place as bishop wearing his monk's robe, sitting on a wooden stool, and carrying his wooden staff for a crozier. At first he lodged in a room off the apse of the church, but the unending interruptions forced him to move to a cave on the outskirts of the town where he was soon joined by others. In time their hillside was honeycombed with cells and they formed a religious community. He shepherded his flock ceaselessly, traveling by foot, by donkey, by boat, until he finally conceived an orderly plan for visiting each settlement by dividing them into what he called *parishes*. We owe the idea of parishes to Martin of Tours.

He cured, healed, counseled, preached; and he traveled all over Gaul converting pagans, interceding for prisoners, rebuking rulers. He was far from home when his last sickness came upon him and at the age of eighty he died. A friend of saints, he was an uncle of another, St. Patrick (through his sister), and he is called the patron, some say the father, of Catholic France.

November 16

Saint Margaret of Scotland
1046–1093

Margaret of Scotland was English, both Norman and Saxon. On her Norman side she was the grandniece of St. King Edward the Confessor and cousin to William of Normandy. She found herself related to still another king of England on her Saxon side when the throne was seized by the Saxon Harold at Edward's death. And then, when William invaded England from Normandy nine months later, and Harold died in the battle of Hastings, Margaret and her brother Edgard, the Saxon pretender, became refugees and fled with their mother and sister to Scotland to the court of King Malcom.

Having intended all along to enter the religious life, Margaret was in due time persuaded by Malcom to abandon her plan and become his queen. She bore him six sons and two daughters. When one of these, Matilda, married

Henry I of England, the blood of both Harold and William the Conqueror mixed again in the royal veins and still does today in Elizabeth II and her family.

Margaret was a lovely queen, beautiful and holy. Married to a boor of a man, illiterate and uncultured, she gentled him past all expectations and he worshiped her. She softened his temper and polished his manners; led him to love justice and mercy, to spend long hours in prayer, and to esteem virtue so tenderly and sorrow for sin so deeply that he often wept as he prayed. Although he could not read, he would examine her books with great care, and if he heard her delight in a particular one, he would often press it to his lips to kiss it, sometimes ordering a craftsman to ornament it for her with gold and gems.

She saw that her children were well brought up, charging the governor of the royal nursery to curb them if they needed it, to spank them if they were naughty—"as frolicsome childhood will be." Thanks to her, after Malcom's death Scotland was ruled by three of its noblest kings, the youngest of them St. King David.

She admonished the wicked to become good and the good to become better. She called for frequent councils on such topics as improper observance of Lent, negligence of the Eucharist, and disrespect for the Lord's day. She built a great church in honor of the Trinity, and provided golden vessels and ornaments to be used in the worship of God. In her own chambers, she established a workshop where a guild of noble ladies decorated vestments with embroideries of silk and golden thread for the divine liturgy.

She encouraged merchants to bring to Scotland fabrics, clothing, ornaments, and precious wares, which up to that time were unknown in that harsh land. It is quite possible that Margaret introduced the Scottish tartans. She brought grace and elegance to the court and nobility to its customs and manners, not for the sake of worldly pleasure but because "duty compelled her to discharge what the kingly dignity required."

But most of all she was famous for her charity to the poor and her redemption of English slaves. When she went out on foot or on horseback, the poor flocked around her, and if she ran out of money, her attendants gave her their money and even their garments in order that no one should go away empty-handed. She pillaged the royal treasury for them, and when the king caught her in the act he only laughed and threatened to have her arrested. When she heard of the presence of Saxon slaves, who were everywhere in bonds after the Norman conquest, she speedily paid their ransom and set them free. She had shelters built for pilgrims near the Church of St. Andrew, and she provided servants to attend them with refreshment and ships to transport them across the water, forbidding that any fee be charged for the crossing.

During Advent and Lent, after a few hours' rest at night, she and the king rose and went to the church to pray. Returning to her chamber, they would wash the feet of six poor persons and give them alms before again retiring. In the morning after prayer, she had nine little orphans brought to her; she took each of them on her knee and fed them with her own spoon—"soft food such as children of their tender age like." When this was done, she went with the king to the royal hall where they alone, unaided by servants, distributed alms to 300 of the poor and served them food and drink. After prayer in the church, and before she ate, she herself waited upon twenty-four poor people whom she supported as long as she lived. Wherever she lived, they lived; when she traveled, they accompanied her. "Not until she had devoutly waited upon Christ in the poor was it her habit to refresh her own feeble body," wrote her confessor, Bishop Turgot. Even then, her fasting was so strenuous that to the end of her life she suffered from "an acute pain in the stomach." Which, nevertheless, he adds, did not impair her strength in good works.

One miracle only seems to be reported. A beautiful book of the Gospels, adorned with gold and precious stones, illustrated with painted and gilded figures, was dropped in a river as they journeyed. It was found hours later lying on the river bed, its leaves in constant motion from the current, its protective silken inserts torn away. But no mark of destruction could be discovered beyond one small water stain inside the cover. (The book can still be seen in the Bodleian Library at Oxford.)

As she lay dying after four years of suffering, she perceived that Malcom and one of her sons had been slain in battle. When Edgar, another, assured her that all was well, she admonished him to tell the truth. She died calmly and tranquily, the bloom of beauty returning to her face. At her request her body was buried opposite the altar in the church she had built, Dunfermline Abbey.

Her biographer and confessor, Bishop Turgot of St. Andrews, wrote: "Not only would she have given to the poor all she possessed; but if she could have done so she would have given away her very self. She was poorer than any of her paupers; for they, even when they had nothing, wished to have something; while all her anxiety was to strip herself of all she had."

November 30

Saint Andrew the Apostle
First Century

A ll we know about St. Andrew the Apostle is found in
eight passages in the Gospels, plus a bit of specula-
tion from tradition. He was evidently born in Bethsaida in
Galilee, bore a Greek name which means *courageous,* and
both he and his brother Simon worked with their father
Jona, who was a fisherman. They lived at Capharnaum on
the lake of Tiberius.

But even the few glimpses we have of Andrew reveal
one of the most appealing members of the Twelve. Andrew had two outstanding characteristics—he did not resent remaining in the background, and he was always taking others to Jesus. Even Peter owed his introduction to
Andrew. As a disciple of John the Baptist, Andrew had
Jesus pointed out to him one day with, "Behold, the lamb
of God!" (Jn. 1:36). Together with a companion, he followed the Lord, and when Jesus noticed the two behind
him, he asked what they wanted. "Where do you live?"
they asked. "Come and see," Jesus replied. And they went
to where he was living and stayed for the whole day. Because John has made this observation in his own text, it is

· 179

supposed that the unnamed companion was John himself, who would have remembered every detail of that memorable day. Returning, Andrew sought out his brother Simon and told him, "We have found the Messiah," and led Simon to him. Now it was enough to stand back and let these two meet.

Never once did Andrew appear within that inner circle of special friends, Peter, James, and John. They were with Jesus at the healing of Jairus's daughter, with him on the Mount of Transfiguration and in the Garden of Gethsemane—but Andrew was not.

Andrew appears again when the Lord is concerned to feed the five thousand. "There is a boy here who has five barley loaves and two fishes," he says, then hesitating at his own presumption, adds, "but what are these among so many?" Philip had said the situation was hopeless, but not Andrew. He searched the crowd looking for something, anything, he wasn't sure what—so he made an act of faith in he didn't know what.

The barley loaves and fishes in this story are full of meaning. Barley bread was the cheapest of all the bread and the most contemptible. The regulation Temple offering of a woman who had committed adultery was a mixture of wine, oil, and barley flour, not wheat, because barley was the food of beasts and her sin was considered the sin of a beast. Barley bread was the food of the poor.

The fishes were a common dish all over the Roman Empire and were no bigger than sardines. In those days, fresh fish were an unheard-of luxury and no one had the means of transporting them very far from the seaside in edible condition. So when these small fish that swarmed in the waters of the Sea of Galilee were caught, they were pickled and made into a kind of savory. Thus the little boy in the story gave to Jesus his picnic lunch, a few pickled fish to help make the dry barley bread taste like something.

Andrew was a man who could not keep Jesus to himself. Not for him the select group of initiates set apart enjoying the man of the hour. He seemed to feel that his own longing for the Messiah was the measure of others' need. Toward the end of the public ministry, it was Andrew who brought the inquiring Greeks to Jesus, those men "whose practice it was to come up to the Feast" (Jn. 12:20–21). Why would they want to meet him? Were they in the court of the Gentiles the day Jesus drove the money-changers out of the Temple and now were anxious to be introduced? They went to Philip (who had a Greek name) and asked, "Sir, we wish to see Jesus," and Philip turned them over to Andrew.

It was Andrew who asked Jesus, when he spoke of the destruction of Jerusalem, "When will these things happen?" (Mk. 13:3–4). Jesus answered by pointing out that the way one lives makes him ready for death and is more important than knowing the hour of death; and he warned him against false teachers. We see Andrew for the last time praying and waiting with the others in the upper room after the Ascension.

What happened afterwards is tradition. The various Acts appear to be apocryphal. Eusebius says he preached in Scythia near the Black Sea; another tradition holds that he went to Greece. St. Gregory Nazianzus mentions Epirus, St. Jerome mentions Achaia. The place and manner of Andrew's death are in doubt as well. The claim that he was bound to a cross saltire (X-shaped) dates only from the fourteenth century. There is another tradition without foundation—that he preached in Kiev, but from it has come his role as patron of Russia. A more credible tradition holds that his relics were transported to Scotland in the fourth century, thus he is also a patron of Scotland, and

it is a tradition to bake shortbread cookies in the shape of an X on his feast day.

St. Andrew is the patron of all those who forget themselves in the joy of knowing the Lord, who do not mind taking second place so others might know him also.

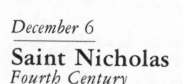

December 6

Saint Nicholas
Fourth Century

There are few saints about whom so little is known, but about whom so many stories have been told, as St. Nicholas. Perhaps in the ages when there was no television or movies, when even books and pictures were rarely the property of the people, and story-telling was the principal entertainment, the life of a saint, embellished and told over a period of time, became so fixed in the memory of generations that the distinction between fact and fancy diminished and one day the mixture of both was written down as "gospel."

This does not mean that St. Nicholas was not real but only that beyond the bare facts of his existence little is known of him. He was born in Patara in the province of Lycia on the southwest coast of Asia Minor, was ordained priest, and when the see of Myra, the capital, became vacant Nicholas was made its bishop and became famous for his piety, his zeal, and his miracles.

The Greek histories of his life maintain that he suffered under the persecution of Diocletian, that he was at the Council of Nicaea and there condemned Arianism. Other lives are silent on these details. He died at Myra, was buried in its cathedral, and in the eleventh century when the Saracens overcame Myra, his relics were removed to Bari, which is why he is also known as St. Nicholas of Bari.

But in the ninth century—five hundred years later—a monk known as St. Methodius of Constantinople, regretting that "the life of this distinguished shepherd has been unknown to the faithful," took it upon himself to inform them of its details. It is from this *Life,* called the least unreliable of them all, and numerous other "lives" that the charming tales of this beloved saint have their origin. If they are not fact, at least they are delightful and have inspired centuries of devotion; and St. Nicholas does not seem to mind all the invention that has gone into them.

For example, there is the claim that the baby Nicholas would nurse at his mother's breast only on Wednesdays and Fridays and only in the evening, as dictated by the rules of fast. His parents were said to have died when he was young, leaving him with an inheritance which he determined to devote to charity. The opportunity soon arose when a man in the town lost all his money and was unable to give his three daughters dowries. Hearing that the father planned to turn them over to a house of ill fame, Nicholas on three occasions, under cover of darkness, tossed three bags of gold in the window of the man's house for the girls. On the final visit, he was discovered by the father who, overwhelmed by such generosity, repented his evil intentions.

The three bags of gold have become the three golden balls over the pawnbroker's shop. The custom of having children set out their shoes on the vigil of his feast, in which the saint puts goodies for the good, straw or coal for the naughty, also has its origin in this story, as does the hanging of stockings on Christmas Eve. Always, then as now, St. Nicholas's generosity is done in Christ's name.

The tale of Nicholas's journey to Jerusalem, the storm at sea during which he miraculously saved the ship—which accounts for devotion to St. Nicholas by seafarers—is, alas, from the story of another Nicholas, the Bishop of Pinara. An eighteenth-century archbishop of Santa Serina is responsible for confusing the two. Other tales include an account of his becoming a boy bishop; the grisly story of the three little boys, murdered and pickled, whom he restored to life (a horrible story for children); and his miraculous rescue of a boy fallen into a well. He is said to have attended the Council of Nicaea where he slapped Arius in the face, was imprisoned for it, and was later rescued by Our Lord and his Blessed Mother. He is also said to have appeared to Constantine to enlist his help in saving three innocent men from execution.

He is probably the best known of all the saints, inspiring even the most hardhearted to generosity toward children and the poor at Christmas—even in his altered identity as Santa Claus. He is a patron saint of children, schoolboys and girls, sailors, Russia, scholars, fishermen, dock workers, coopers, brewers, travelers, pilgrims, and those who have unjustly lost law suits. He is invoked against robbers and is sometimes said to be the patron of pickpockets and thieves—surely the reformed ones or those whom he is about to reform.

Saint Ambrose
c. 339–397

St. Ambrose was born in Trèves (Trier, in West Germany) about the year 339, the youngest of three children, all of whom became saints. At his father's death, his mother, Marcellina, returned to Rome where she took vows. There Ambrose, age twelve, and his brother Satyrus began studies preparatory to following a career in law like their illustrious father. Ambrose rose so rapidly to prominence that by thirty he was appointed governor of two provinces, with his residence in Milan, then the capital of the Roman Empire. He ruled with such distinction that at the death of the Arian bishop of Milan, he was asked to preside at the election of a new bishop. As he spoke to the people about the voting, a voice cried out from the crowd: "Ambrose for bishop!"

Astonished, Ambrose protested. He had no wish to be bishop; he was not even baptized. One account, hardly credible, tells that to dissuade the people he pretended improper behavior. In the end, he was put under house arrest, the emperor was consulted, heartily concurred with the choice, and eight days later at the age of thirty-four, Ambrose was baptized, received the proper ecclesiastical orders, and was consecrated bishop.

Having been catapulted into the sanctuary without any theological background, he began to study assiduously.

Augustine describes him in his house, surrounded by people seeking his help and counsel, and reading whenever he had time. He preached gloriously, wrote, ate but once a day in the evening, and then penned his own sermons because he did not want to keep his secretaries up all night. He gave away his money to the poor, keeping only what he needed for his sister and himself, and he eventually had church vessels melted down to pay ransom for Roman captives.

Perhaps more familiar for his role in the conversion of St. Augustine than as a Father of the Church, Ambrose was one of the first Marian theologians and wrote, among many other things, the first work on the Holy Spirit. Because he drew from Basil and Athanasius, Jerome made the sour and unfair accusation that Ambrose "decked himself like a jackdaw with other birds' plumes and spoiled the good things he stole from the Greeks."

A splendid administrator, Ambrose was equally fearless in rebuking the mighty when necessary, and the first of such contests was with the Empress Justina. Milan was entirely Catholic by the time the thirteen-year-old Valentinian ascended the throne under the regency of his Arian mother Justina. Her first demand of him was that one of the city's churches be given to the Arians, not so much for a place of worship as to raise Arianism to the level of Christianity. Ambrose refused and was vociferously supported by the people. When Valentinian's chamberlain, a eunuch, threatened to behead Ambrose, he replied with what is surely one of the saltiest lines handed down from the Fathers: "Then I shall suffer as befits a bishop, and you will act as befits a eunuch."

Justina tried to entrap Ambrose again by dictating an edict granting free assembly to Arians in any church whatsoever. He opposed it, and she ended up barricading him and his people in the basilica. It was during this siege that

Ambrose initiated the practice of chanting the psalms antiphonally in two choirs, and taught the people some of his own beautiful Ambrosian hymns (for this he shares with St. Hilary the distinction of being the father of Latin hymnology). Among the crowd keeping vigil with him was Monica, the mother of Augustine. In a great sermon at the end of their ordeal, he uttered the famous retort: "The emperor is within the church, not above it," a distinction the rulers of Christendom had yet to learn. Just thirty-five years before, at the Council of Arles, Contantius II had said to the bishops: "My will *is* canon law."

Justina, betrayed by a usurper, now fled with Valentinian and his sister Galla to the eastern empire for refuge with their general, Theodosius, who married Galla and at the death of Justina became coemperor with Valentinian. Here at last was an emperor who was orthodox, devoutly Catholic, and the bishop's confidant and friend. It augured well.

Their first clash came when Theodosius ordered the Christians in a small town in Macedonia to rebuild a synagogue they had destroyed. Whether Ambrose resented his disregard of church jurisdiction in the affair or was actually in the wrong is not clear, but he rebuked the emperor publicly in a sermon and Theodosius was angered. He determined not to take the bishop into his political confidence henceforth, which was largely responsible for the horrible event at Thessalonica. There a local commandant had imprisoned a popular charioteer for immorality and would not release him for the games. Enraged, the sports fans murdered the commandant, and Theodosius, in a savage temper, considered massacre as a punishment. Ambrose heard about it and intervened, but the emperor gave the command nevertheless. He immediately countermanded it but it was too late. The soldiers at the garrison waited until the amphitheatre was filled with people, locked the gates, and slew all seven thousand, innocent as well as guilty, in one of the bloodiest massacres in history.

Ambrose, horrified, prayed for wisdom, and when the emperor appeared at the cathedral, refused to celebrate the holy sacrifice in his presence. Warning him of possible excommunication, he declared that not until Theodosius laid aside his imperial ornaments and sat in the place for public penitents would he be allowed to attend the liturgy. Theodosius did, weeping for his sins, and his people weeping with him. Finally, the following Christmas, he was welcomed once more to the Lord's table. Afterwards, he would say, "I know no one except Ambrose who deserves the name of bishop."

Ambrose's greatest contribution to the church was not his writing, which lacked the originality and brilliance of others of the fathers, but his modeling of the role of bishop. By his faith, goodness, and disinterested self-denial he became a bulwark of both his nation and the church. He restored to Italy a firm and true faith which would spread outward to the very limits of Christendom. He was a bastion of defense, witnessing to Christ before kings and showing how weak was imperial despotism before the power of spiritual strength—a living example of Paul's phrase: "When I am weak, then I am strong." He was a spiritual ruler, a devoted statesman, a faithful servant, a paternal adviser, the kind of great man whose door was open to whoever needed him—and to whom, in Christ, everyone was equal.

Dying, he refused to pray for his own recovery, saying ". . . I am not afraid to die, for Our Lord is good." He died on Easter Eve in the year 397 at the age of fifty-seven, burnt out in the service of the church.

December 13

Saint Lucy
Died 304

Nothing is known about St. Lucy beyond the fact that she was a fourth-century martyr whose name was placed in the Canon of the Mass by St. Gregory the Great in the seventh century. It was an English bishop named St. Adhelm who, evidentaly unaware that the acts of her martyrdom were fictitious, wrote the story that has been told of her ever since. Legend it may be, but it has made Lucy beloved to her devotees and has produced so many beautiful symbols and customs that it bears retelling. It goes like this.

St. Lucy was born in Sicily, in the city of Syracuse, of noble and wealthy Christian parents. While still a young girl, she offered her virginity to God, but kept this a secret from her widowed mother who, in time, tried to press Lucy into marrying a young pagan admirer. It was only after Lucy's mother was cured of a recurring hemorrhage, after praying at the tomb of St. Agatha, that in gratitude she heard Lucy's request and granted it.

The time was during the persecution of Diocletian, and her angry suitor, furious to be rejected, reported Lucy as a

Christian to the local officials. Brought before the judge, she was ordered to recant, and when she refused she was condemned to a house of ill fame. But when the guards came to take her away, she could not be moved, not even when oxen were brought to drag her. An attempt to burn her was futile, and finally the enraged magistrate was said to cry out, "Why don't you burn?" To which Lucy replied, "To bear witness to my true spouse, Jesus Christ, I do not burn." Only when a sword was put to her throat did she finally die.

There are numerous variations of the story. One tells that Lucy, especially esteemed for her beautiful eyes, had more than one admirer, and to dissuade all such suitors she put out her own eyes. This accounts for the statues of Lucy holding her eyes on a silver platter, and the fact that she is invoked by people with diseases of the eye.

She endeared herself so to the missionaries who went north to preach the Gospel that in time she became a special favorite among the Christians of Scandinavia. A familiar Swedish custom on her feast is the celebration of The Lucy Bride. On the evening of the feast, one maiden from the parish is chosen to be St. Lucy and together with her attendants, wearing white garments and carrying martyrs' palms, she enters the church bearing on her head a crown set with candleholders and lighted candles. Thus Lucy, whose name comes from the Latin word for "light" (lux) is the Advent saint whose feast points in a special way to the coming of the Light of the World on Christmas.

A Hungarian custom is to plant Christmas wheat on St. Lucy's feast. Pressed gently into a pot of garden soil, watered and kept in a moderately warm place, the wheat will sprout soft and green by Christmas. Children carry it to the crêche as a symbol of the Eucharistic bread which celebrates the union of all Christians to Christ and to one another.

This is the time of year when our Jewish brothers celebrate their Feast of Hannukah, which is also called the Feast of Lights and was one of the feasts that Jesus would have celebrated in his home. It recalls the victory of Judas Maccabeus over the Syrians who had won many of the Israelites to idol worship and had laid waste to the Holy City (1 Mac. 4:36–59).

Led by Judas Maccabeus, the Jews triumphed over their enemies and set about purifying and refurbishing the Temple which had been despoiled. It is the solemnity of the Dedication of the Temple which is celebrated at Hannukah. An ancient tradition tells that on returning to the Temple, the Jews found only one small jar of holy oil left for the sacred lamps but they burned miraculously for eight days until new oil could be obtained. Its name, Feast of Lights, comes from the custom of lighting eight candles, a new one each day, for the duration of the feast. Children receive a little present each day at the lighting of the candles.

Hannukah, indeed, is not "the Jewish Christmas," and it is disturbing to our brothers the Jews to have it treated so. But as a feast of lights, it comes at a time of the year when we too think and speak and symbolize our faith with light. The Feast of St. Lucy and the Feast of Hannukah in December can remind us that we worship the same God and pray for his light to be shed on the same world.

December 23

Saint John
of Kanty
(St. John Cantius)
1390–1473

This St. John was born in the little village of Kanty in the Diocese of Krakow in Poland, the son of a pious country couple named Stanislaus and Anne. Quick and bright, the boy was sent to primary school, then to the academy in Krakow, and there, at the encouragement of his professors, he enrolled at the university. He was a good student, took several degrees, decided to enter the priesthood, and upon ordination was appointed to a lectureship in Scripture.

From the very beginning of his priesthood, the two characteristics of John Kanty were the simplicity and asceticism of his life and his love for the poor. He lived so abstemiously that his superiors cautioned him about the dangers to his health, but John only pointed out that the Fathers of the Desert had lived even more rigorously and lasted to ripe old age. A famous story is told of his sitting at the table in the dining hall of the university one evening when he saw a famished-looking beggar pass by the door. Jumping up, he took his food to the man and when he returned, it was said, his plate was miraculously refilled.

192 ·

The occasion was long commemorated at the university by setting aside a special meal for a poor man every day.

As so often happens, John's scholarship and holiness inspired as much envy as admiration, and his rivals at the university managed to get him removed and sent as pastor to a small country parish at Olkusz. He approached the new role obediently but was filled with trepidation, convinced that he was ill-equipped to bear the burdens of ministry in a parish. His parishioners were only too quick to show that they did not want him. But he persevered, and when at last he was recalled to Krakow, the people had grown so to love him that they followed him out of town grieving. He scolded them. "This sadness does not please God. If I have done any good for you in all these years, then sing a song of joy!"

His second appointment to the university was to a chair in Scripture which he held until the end of his life. He left such a reputation for learning and holiness that for many years after his death his doctoral gown was used to vest each candidate at the conferring of academic degrees.

But even as he became famous for his learned accomplishments and was a welcome guest at the tables of the nobles, concern for the poor remained first in his heart. He had few possessions, so freely did he give things to the needy. On one occasion he appeared for dinner at an elegant household in such a shabby cassock that the servants turned him away at the door. He went home and changed, and when a dish was spilled on his clothes during the meal he said, "Never mind; my clothes deserve some dinner since it was to them I owe the pleasure of being here at all."

He slept on the floor, never ate meat, and made four pilgrimages to Rome on foot carrying his belongings on his back. He even made a pilgrimate to Jerusalem, secretly hoping to become a martyr among the Turks.

He told his students, "Fight all false opinions, but let your weapons be patience, sweetness, and love. Roughness is bad for your soul and spoils the best cause." When he was dying, and the news reached the people of Krakow, grief was universal. "Never mind about this prison which is decaying," he said of his body, "but think of the soul that is going to leave it!" He died on Christmas Eve, 1473, and was canonized in 1767.

Families who would like to share an exciting adventure with St. John Kanty in medieval Poland will enjoy reading the great classic, *The Trumpeter of Krakow* by Eric P. Kelly, a tale of heroism and grace as splendid today as it was when it was first written.

St. John Kanty is a Christmas saint and in his honor families might imitate the beautiful Polish custom of setting a place for the Christ child and his mother at the festive meal on Christmas Eve—perhaps a custom St. John Kanty observed in his own home and which nourished his love for Christ's poor.